WHAT EVERY MAN WISHES HIS FATHER HAD TOLD HIM

Byron Forrest Yawn

HARVEST HOUSE PUBLISHERS

EUGENE, OREGON

All Scripture quotations are taken from the New American Standard Bible®, © 1960, 1962, 1963, 1968, 1971, 1972, 1973, 1975, 1977, 1995 by The Lockman Foundation. Used by permission. (www.Lockman.org)

Cover by Koechel Peterson & Associates, Inc., Minneapolis, Minnesota

Cover photo © iStockphoto/Thinkstock

Back cover author photo by Krystal Mann

Published in association with Patti M. Hummel, President/Agent, Benchmark Group LLC, Nashville, TN. benchmarkgroup1@aol.com.

WHAT EVERY MAN WISHES HIS FATHER HAD TOLD HIM
Copyright © 2012 by Byron Forrest Yawn
Published by Harvest House Publishers
Eugene, Oregon 97402
www.harvesthousepublishers.com

Library of Congress Cataloging-in-Publication Data
Yawn, Byron Forrest.
    What every man wishes his father had told him / Byron Forrest Yawn.
      p. cm.
    ISBN 978-0-7369-4638-4 (pbk.)
    ISBN 978-0-7369-4640-7 (eBook)
    1. Christian men—Religious life. I. Title.
    BV4528.2.Y39 2012
    248.8'42—dc23

                                 2011021194

Printed in the United States of America

        12 13 14 15 16 17 18 19 20 / BP-SK / 10 9 8 7 6 5 4 3 2 1

To my sons Wade, Zachary, and Blake

and

my beloved father, Dr. Victor Wade Yawn II

Post Tenebrus Lux

CONTENTS

FOREWORD BY JOHN MACARTHUR

I n ancient biblical cultures it was understood that every father had a solemn duty to help usher his sons into manhood. He fulfilled that role by teaching them wisdom, instructing them in the facts of life, preparing them for the disciplines of adulthood, and indoctrinating them in the way of truth and righteousness. That kind of fatherly training is exemplified in the Old Testament book of Proverbs—paternal and spiritual wisdom preserved for us in pithy, memorable statements that are easy to digest, powerfully practical, and profoundly wise.

Children in those days entered adulthood and were expected to assume grown-up responsibilities at a much younger age than contemporary Western cultures have grown accustomed to. There was no concept of "adolescence"—that troublesome phase of drawn-out immaturity and rebellion today's young people are expected to splash around in for several years following puberty. In biblical times, adulthood came early. That pattern is reflected in the Jewish celebration of Bar Mitzvah at age 13, when boys become "sons of commandment" and are formally recognized as having come of age. The same approach is also seen in the maturing of Christ into manhood. The only record of Jesus' teenage years is a single verse, telling us that He "kept increasing in wisdom and in stature, and in favor with God and man" (Luke 2:52). He personified steady growth into manhood; He was not hindered or diverted from that goal by any of the typical distractions of youth.

In stark contrast to the biblical pattern, young men in our culture today begin to manifest adolescent characteristics (such as rebellion, depression, and chronic cynicism) earlier than ever—and they remain immature longer than ever. Some, it seems, never do become true men. In fact, many become fathers without ever really becoming adults.

No wonder. Permanent adolescence is relentlessly romanticized and shamelessly encouraged in practically all popular entertainment and advertising. Manhood itself is often strongly discouraged, while society's fundamental values are systematically being feminized. Trends such as those have given rise to an epidemic of fatherless homes and irresponsible thirty-something males. Countless young men are addicted to entertainment, living in a culture already shaped to a very large degree by movies, video games, and fantasy role-playing. It is frankly no surprise that real men are in such scarce supply. Never has there been a more urgent need for wise and diligent fathers.

Many people have noticed these cultural shifts, of course, including some Christian leaders. Evangelical attempts to address the decline of manhood have gone to two extremes—one side encouraging the church to embrace feminist values; the other side promoting a radically cartoonish caricature of manhood. (One wildly popular approach encourages Christian men to treat fantasy characters as role models.) The fact that evangelical leaders and best-selling authors would put such unbiblical suggestions on the table is of course part of the problem.

Byron Yawn has a much better suggestion. It starts with listening to what the Bible says about manhood—letting Scripture shape our value system, our view of masculinity, and our lifestyles as true men and true disciples of Christ. Specifically, Pastor Yawn points out that the quintessential model of perfect manhood is not a fictional character from a gladiator movie; not a soft, epicene trendoid with exaggerated postmodern sensitivities; and not a bullying tyrant who mistakes intimidation for authority. The archetype and epitome of everything a mature man should be is Jesus Christ.

That's precisely what Ephesians 4:13 says: The measure of "a mature man" is "the stature which belongs to the fullness of Christ." That's also the theme and central lesson of this book.

Pastor Yawn has done a considerable amount of careful thinking about manhood as it is portrayed in Scripture. He writes poignantly, straightforwardly, compellingly about what it means to be a man, about how fathers can train their sons to be true men, and about how sons can honor their fathers in a manly fashion. This is a refreshing, challenging, engaging, and (best of all) biblical study of a subject that has too often been overlooked, handled badly, or looked at through the lens of cultural rather than biblical values. Byron Yawn makes none of those mistakes. The result is a book that will be treasured by fathers and sons alike.

IN PURSUIT OF
BIBLICAL MANHOOD

Dad, you and I are just alike, except for the nose hairs.
{ BLAKE ALEXANDER YAWN }

*He said, "Take now your son, your only son, whom you love, Isaac,
and go to the land of Moriah; and offer him there as a burnt offering on
one of the mountains of which I will tell you."
So Abraham rose early in the morning and saddled his donkey...*
{ GENESIS 22:2-3 }

T his book strikes out in three simultaneous directions. First, it heads backward to a place just before the dawn of time in a young boy's life. A point of innocence and nostalgia complete with action figures (not figurines), baseball mitts, and plastic guns. The very moment when someone—otherwise known as dad—should have stepped in and started preparing that young man for the mind-bending realities dead ahead. For many, if not most of us, this was a season of missed opportunity. What we struggled to figure out at twenty-eight could have been generally explained at eight. It would have taken only a few minutes of time to condescend to a boy's level and show him the way. At least we could have seen it coming when it ran us over.

Second, it rises up above our present circumstance and allows us to survey our person from a slightly higher elevation. From the high ground of the cross the lines of our current struggles can be traced back to their beginning. The root of recurring aches common to every man and uniquely situated in each life can be seen from a better vantage point. As we look down on our own life we may finally catch a glimpse of what's been causing all the trouble. We can see freedom from here.

Third, it reaches forward. It reaches out a hand to those nostalgic creatures running all around us. Those boys enjoying the leisure of their childhood who can't imagine the mountain of experiences ahead of them. Those adolescent males caught in the drift of changes no one could ever anticipate. It's a hand of hope reaching down to the next generation of men. There is an opportunity to do for them what was never done for us. To introduce them to a freedom in Christ that is able to blaze a trail out of all the confusion. "Dear son, there is a way to live, and you can live it."

To the adult son who looks back and regrets, there is hope. To the confused husband who looks down on his life with despair, there is a means to victory. To the father who looks ahead to the future of his own children, there is a way. In every case it is the Lord Jesus Christ.

These essays are glimpses into the real-time struggles of any ordinary man's heart. They depict some of the rough terrain that leads up to biblical masculinity. In many instances I had to look no farther than my own life—mostly failure—for inspiration. Then there were the many noble lives of men near me who have lived so well. In the end I have only tried to say what most men are thinking.

The intent is to force a man to the foot of the cross and back again upon his own soul in light of it. I deliberately push away from any variation on the ever-present twelve-step approach to life-change and manhood. There are specific reasons I avoid this genre. First, life is not that easy. Change is not convenient. The narcissistic bent of our culture naïvely assumes a book can solve our issues. We are a trend-ready church. Change is a matter of grace, not cleverness. I offer ideas. You apply them.

Second, men naturally want steps. They like to tinker. They like steps simply because they're easy. Real repentance and deep introspection is much more painful. The church has already suffered enough from decades of over-principlization. We have an endless offering of packaged approaches with little or no results to show for it. The recent history of evangelicalism can be charted by the numerous "pretty books" that line men's shelves. Eventually, they are released as leather-bound journals and then it's off to the graveyard of all Christian crazes—garage sales. Men need to think, not grasp at straws.

Coming to terms with biblical manhood is challenging. The Bible offers no concise definition. It assumes it. I suppose this is because it's obvious. Only a fallen humanity could confuse it so drastically. The church has tried to provide clarity, but the definitions are all over the page. Some are Pollyanna. They have no connection to the travails of modern culture. It's impossible to live up to the polyester standards. Others miss the mark by miles, either directly or indirectly neutering men in the church. They rob biblical spirituality of any sense of masculinity. Men can't be real men in the church. No real man wants to go this direction. Still others have gone too far in their reaction to the androgynous spirituality affecting the church. They have confused John Rambo with Jesus Christ. A real man will see the childishness of such depictions. All of this has barely been helpful in the recovery of a clear understanding.

I've read many books and articles on manhood in preparation for this offering. One observation in my research has astounded me. In the vast majority of cases, Jesus Christ is barely mentioned and often never directly put forward as the example of biblical manhood. The chapters are few that extol the Savior as the prime meridian of masculinity. We turn to heroic biblical figures and icons of cinematic history, but not to Christ. Yet Christ is the place to which all biblical figures point and the one man who makes Hollywood depictions of strength look foolish. There is no understanding of manhood without first understanding Christ.

The only thing more astounding than this silence on Christ in Christian literature on manhood is my own failure in turning to Him. Jesus is obvious. He is not assumed by the Bible. He is what every Christian man should desire to be. He is our Lord. We can look to Him and see manhood in its purest form. We need Him.

Some have given up trying to be men and have settled into the haziness of boyhood instead. Emotionally, they are still somewhere in their mom's basement. They lurk in the weeds of mediocrity afraid of growing up. Wives are more like nannies. Others, frustrated by the disappointment of their lives, have shut down. They survive behind hearts of stone. Mean and surly. They've never known the joy of being a servant leader. They can't see the point in enjoying the souls around them. Wives are more like enemies. My heart is big toward both.

Then there are those who are tired of mailing it in. They are looking for that hand to lift them out of the weeds and quarries. These men excite my soul. They give me great hope for families and churches. When I think of them, words come easy. Too many have made a mockery of manhood. No doubt there's a lot of failure. But has anyone ever offered a biblical and realistic solution? This book, meager as it is, is my attempt at helping.

There is a lot of straight talk in these pages. It's necessary if we're going to confront the little boy hiding in all of us. It's how I talk. It's no different from how my friends and I confront each other in real time. The elders, staff, and men I serve with at Community Bible Church cut each other no slack and are large on grace. I find it refreshing. Most men do when they encounter it.

There've been enough passes handed out already. We tiptoe around each other's insecurities like we're managing a minefield. That's not friendship. That's codependency. So I try to step on everyone I can along the way. If your feelings are hurt, they probably needed to be.

If you think I'm wrong, there's probably some truth to your observation. I remind you the title is *What Every Man Wishes His Father Had Told Him* and not *Everything Every Man Should Have Ever Been Told*.

If you appreciate something I write, I remind you as well that even a blind hog can root out an acorn from time to time. In the end, if I'm going to be transparent and put myself out there, I'm taking you down with me. Soul searching is not easy, but it is the path to freedom.

You will not agree with everything I say. This is especially true as you compare my observations to those of pop psychology, which have now become axiomatic in our experiences. I'm no big fan of the clichés we confidently toss around assuming they solve all our issues with cleverness. But I would challenge you to examine all these urban legends afresh. Is what we have assumed about our severest struggles and deepest needs as men accurate? Or have these answers been fashioned to let us off the hook? Should we drag our sinful hearts up to the cross of Christ would the assessment be different? Would it use different words to describe us? Sin instead of addiction. Corruption instead of disadvantage.

I believe the gospel clarifies and applies to all of life with ongoing and ever-increasing relevance. It applies to the specifics. This includes manhood. The gospel is not just a starting point. It is the length and breadth of the Christian life as well. Not to give away the ending, but this book basically presses various issues about manhood and masculinity through the filter of the gospel. This is the gospel *and manhood*. Genius, right? Not even.

There is a revival of gospel clarity taking place in the church at this very moment in time. I've merely capitalized on others' clarity. We've come back around to the cross. The cross is glorious. It's rather embarrassing to realize how far from it we've wandered over the years. The gospel always seems to hide from the church in the wide open. We miss it. We look past it. It's always there beckoning us back from our moralism and pragmatism. As I say herein, it is usually the last place we turn. It should be the first. Masculinity can never make sense without it.

For years I mocked that bumper sticker that reads "Real Men Love Jesus." At the time I considered it an oversimplification at best and evidence of our slogan-driven spirituality at worst. I once saw it posted on a billboard as I drove down a highway with my family. It was strategically situated over a gentlemen's club. It seemed a foolish gesture. Are we to believe that Jesus can save us from the brazen immorality in our culture? Yes. We must believe it or there is nothing to believe. The more I've peered at manhood through the cross, the more I've come to admit the truth of this simple statement. If men would love Jesus they would be real men. If men would love Jesus they would find a power over the most notorious sins. Real men do love Jesus. Real men would have the courage to take a bullet for the gospel. Real men always have.

I had an English professor in college confront me with one of the most vivid definitions of courage I've ever encountered. As the story goes, there's a man who sees a child playing on some train tracks at the very moment a train is about to overtake it. The man jumps in front of the train at the last minute and saves the child. He is instantly heralded a hero by those who witness his act. His face appears in the local paper and he is lauded far and wide for his courage. But is that really courage? Would not most anyone make that move in that instant?

Imagine the same man. This time he is approached by a stranger who informs him that in exactly one week at a specific time a child will be playing on the same set of tracks. The child will be unaware of the impending danger of the oncoming train. If this man so chooses, he may throw himself in front of that train a mere second before it overtakes the innocent child. But there is no guarantee of survival.

Then that same man walks away and has an entire week to ponder the possible terrifying consequences of doing the right thing. The loss of his life. The loss of the child's life. A widowed wife. Orphaned children. Or maybe unthinkable injuries. Maybe paralysis. The excruciating pain of tons of steel and heat dashing his body.

After a week passes he stands before those same tracks, having had all that time to contemplate the cost of doing the right thing, and jumps. In that instant, he weighed fully the cost of serving someone—ultimate self-sacrifice. That is courage. Courage does not head toward preferable outcomes. Courage acts even in the face of consequences simply because it is the right thing to do.

Biblical manhood requires such courage. I don't intend to be overly dramatic here. It's not as if we're carrying around the nuclear codes or cutting wires on atomic bombs. We're merely leading wives, raising children, and serving the gospel of Christ. You know, simple stuff. But the devil hates simple stuff. Especially men who are good at it. This is exactly why it takes courage. The world and the devil attack unimpeachable godliness from every angle. Humble godly men are the devil's worst enemy.

It takes nerve to be a man who loves Jesus in this God-hating culture. There are real consequences for acting at the right moment. It calls us to a hundred daily deaths. There are innumerable moments we throw ourselves in front of pain for others. It's a daily death to self. Manhood is not what we've been led to believe. Men are self-sacrificing lovers of a living God. Dear God, bring us leaders.

The practical ministry of the church rests on the lives of courageous godly men. Men who take the truth seriously, but themselves not too seriously. What the church needs are warriors of the gospel of Christ, not boys trapped in men's bodies. Gospel ministry on the local church level begins with men. No pastor is truly leading if he is not raising them up.

That parable of courage and the train finds its antitype in Jesus Christ. The Bible makes it abundantly clear that Jesus knew full well the consequences of obedience to the Father. Yet with an eternity to ponder infinite suffering He offered Himself as a sacrifice for my sin. Essentially throwing Himself in front of the Father's wrath for a sinner like me. In this moment, masculinity finds its fullest definition.

He is the one and only son offered who spared Abraham's promised son. As He is my Savior, I pray He is the son offered for both of mine.

Byron Forrest Yawn
Nashville, TN

THE SPACE WHERE A DAD SHOULD BE

Then Joseph fell on his father's face,
and wept over him and kissed him.

{ GENESIS 50:1 }

W hat kind of relationship did you have with your father?" And a thousand little memories flood the mind of a son. Immediately a forty-one-year-old husband and father of three is eight again. Few questions have the force to stop grown men in their tracks as does this one. The feelings run deep here. I mean really deep. I asked it of a rather spry waiter once to prove its power to a friend. The waiter was so struck by the apparent insight into his life he was inclined to lie down in the booth opposite me and assume the fetal position. Ask someone yourself. You'll see what I mean. It evokes either warm reminiscent smiles or deeply resentful gazes. It opens a window into a soul. Fathers are important. I mean really important.

Maybe the best answer thus far has been "Good, but not much." Which means, of course, Dad was a good man but not readily available. In the vast majority of cases, however, the answer is not even this favorable. Rare is the smile. Disappointment reigns. Some dads were "merely" negligent. Some were too busy. Some were passive. Some were mute. Some were angry. Some were physically abusive. Some were decent. Some were shells. Some vanished. In nearly every case—even in the worst-case scenarios—the answers are tilted toward gracious and affable. They're more like excuses than answers. Sons have an instinct to cover their fathers' failures. Sons love their dads even when their dads did not love them. It's part of being a son. It's also a sign of how sons are doomed to mimic their fathers' primary failure—*denial*.

If you're in the minority that considers your dad's impact as generally favorable, I'd have you ask a deeper question. Was your dad simply around, or was he actually engaged in your life? There's a big difference. One is a figure. The other is a mentor. How many life lessons did your dad actually offer you? How many principles did he offer when you were eight that you remembered when you were twenty-eight? How many of us had dads who were observant enough to step in and guide our hearts, or facilitate our calling in life? Maybe your dad taught you how to manage money, or instilled a work ethic. But did he teach you how proper money management and a work ethic are tied to much bigger realities? Did he expose you to the deeper joys of such virtues?

Many men will insist their dad's inattention has had no great effect on them. Trust me—they're lying. Boys need fathers like trees need trunks. I've seen strong and sturdy sixty-year-old men weep in sight of the empty space where a dad should have been or at the indelible marks left by tyrants who posed as fathers. So much in a man's life can be traced back to the father—good and bad.

YOU'RE NOT CRAZY

A prime example is the epidemic struggle with sexual sin among Christian men. Oftentimes, when helping men deal with this sin, I will ask, "Did you receive any instruction on sex in your adolescence?" In almost every case the answer is no. Your dad may have offered a single awkward lecture on anatomy, but that's barely even helpful. Mainly we (the church) give the impression that sexuality and the natural desires of young men (or women) are something to be ashamed of. Is it any wonder it's such a pervasive problem? When MTV is teaching our sons everything they know about sex and how to value women, they're doomed.

At the exact moment a young man faces the most substantial physical, emotional, hormonal, and social changes of his life, he's left to figure it out for himself. We stay on them about cleaning their rooms, but don't say a word to them about sex. They go to bed dreaming of Legos in their childhoods and wake up Sasquatch. No one warns them of what's coming. No one does them the incredible favor of assuring them that this bizarre physical transformation is normal. They grow up thinking they're crazy.

In the absence of a guide it's impossible to maneuver this space and live to tell about it. An unsupervised adolescent boy doesn't have a prayer in this culture. You might as well drop him off at the porn shop on his thirteenth birthday. Seriously. Point is, in most cases this struggle (and many others) in men can be traced back to the empty space a father was designed to fill. Is it any wonder adult sons are so resentful of their fathers?

FATHER WOUNDS

At the same time, there are way too many "men" blaming their personal issues on their fathers' failures. You can justify almost anything by lifting up your psyche and showing people your "daddy wound." I know of men who've abandoned their wives and families and offer their "wounded spirits" as justification. At present, blaming our hangups on our "father wounds" is the default position. It's trendy to have one. Like psychological tattoos. They all read, "Dad hurt my feelings." The expression "father wound" is now in the realm of Christian clichés. Which means…it's virtually meaningless.

Nonetheless, deep behind the lines of "suburbianity" this psychosomatic phenomenon is assumed to be true. Men eat it up. You mention the concept to fresh ears and to them, it magically explains the origin of every flaw they've ever had. Some of the most popular books on men are perched on this singular conviction. It's always a pleasant little journey from assumption to foregone conclusion.

Just consider the number of men's Bible studies and accountability groups dedicated to this concept. Men sit around and discuss it for weeks on end, sounding more like girls than men. There's no way this is healthy. What good does it do to incessantly identify a chronic ache without taking action to correct it? It does no good. It makes us more self-absorbed than we already are. Trust me—the men in your small group may be nodding in affirmation on the outside, but they're rolling the eyes of their heart on the inside. They're tired of hearing about your dad's lack of affection.

I get it. I'm not suggesting there's no truth to the concept of emotional wounds. Some of us had messed-up childhoods. I have friends with painful stories. In some instances their personal suffering was so intense it's hard to relate. Comparatively, my dad never beat me with a half-inch thick branch or made me sleep under my bed so as not to hear me sob. Some dads are pure evil. Generally, all of our dads made mistakes and had moments (or decades) of angry excesses. No man is perfect, and others are as far from it as possible.

Honestly though, so what? Get in line. Who hasn't been hurt or sinned against—even by people we're hard-wired to trust? Should we ask our wives about the innumerable "stupid wounds" they've received at our hands? Or should we talk to our kids? Or do we want to compare wounds with the Savior of sinners? This planet is littered with fallen narcissistic scavengers (including you and me) who'll do almost anything to get what they want. Besides, if we were as angry at our sin as we are with our dad, we might actually get past some stuff. By the third (or ten thousandth) sad retelling of our disadvantaged youth, what good has it done anyway?

WHAT THE CROSS SAYS TO VICTIMS

There's a fine line between blame and acceptance. The balance between focusing on the injustices in our life and taking personal responsibility for our lives is difficult. Many men are imprisoned by memories, or the lack thereof. They can't make it past the inequity of their experiences. The solution here is mainly theological and not therapeutic. It's a matter of focus. My point is, it's not about becoming intimate with your hang-ups. It's about becoming intimate with your Creator. Will you spend your days examining self, or something greater than yourself? Other men with equally painful memories have found freedom in the cross. They have a different type of internal struggle. They can't get over the "inequity" of Christ's death.

What's most notable about this last category of people is their normalcy. They're stable, grateful, and productive people who love Christ. They seem never to draw attention to the scars etched in their lives, but are simultaneously better people because of them.

Those who adhere too tightly to the father wound philosophy tend to approach life as victims. Victims of their circumstances. In some cases childhood memories serve as the basic justification for their own misbehavior and delinquency. "Someone hurt me; therefore, you must cut me slack as I destroy everything in my path." Life is spent examining their wounds ad nauseam. Daddy wounds are like rocks in their shoes.

This outlook on life is why some men never grow up. It's an excuse for immobility and failure. They have trendy haircuts at fifty, frustrated wives, wear skinny jeans (strangely resembling elves), discontented jobs, massive debt, still shop at the Gap, try way too hard to be hip, and every single conversation you have with them is about them and why they are still living in their mother's basement emotionally. It's hopeless.

The other perspective has God and the cross in view. It takes in the same pain from a completely different angle. The cross looms over and brings clarity to the trauma that creeps into every life. It alone explains the real reason people do the horrible things they do—*they're sinners*. This perspective requires humility because it acknowledges the mystery of sin. Who can explain why sin causes people to do the things they do? No one. Sin is intentional and irrational at the same time. People do these things because it's in their natures to do them as sinners. But, rather than ending in fatalism, this awareness frees us. It keeps us from fixating our attention on the *why* of our circumstances. This world is sinful, that's *why* people do the things they do.

The cross promises all the abused and abandoned that there will be justice. No one gets away. But, the cross goes farther. It doesn't let the "victims" off the hook either. We've all sinned against people. Everyone has made a victim of someone. The cross is essentially screaming this at humanity. We're all bad people. God did not die to save us from our daddy wounds. He died to save us from ourselves and the consequences of who we are. He died because rescuing sinful humanity from the wrath of God required a brutal death. We're brutal people. This fact brings our self-fulfilling unending therapy session to an abrupt close. Before God we're no better than our abusive, negligent, or "good, but not much" fathers.

Furthermore, the cross proves that our greatest need is not psychological and/or therapeutic, but spiritual. Understanding our circumstances, backgrounds, or psychological makeup may be helpful as far as it goes, but it can't change your heart. It won't help you truly forgive because it begins with an imperfect standard—*you*. The cross presents us with the perfect standard. It's the truth about it all. The greatest tragedy in human history is the death of Christ. The innocent Son of God died in the place of guilty sinners. He was brutalized at the hands of ungrateful rebels. In this sense, the only innocent victim on the planet is Christ. The rest of us—all of us—are guilty. The cross puts the spikes in each of our hands and makes us face the truth about who we are.

From the view of the cross our forgiveness of others is based on the infinitely greater standard. We forgive in view of the forgiveness we've received in Christ. Our willingness to release others is not based on our pathetic self-estimation. It's true forgiveness. It comes from a heart that has been transformed and is being transformed by a growing awareness of the grace of God toward sinners in the cross of Christ. It comes from a life that has been set free from a defense of self. The cross proves unequivocally that there's nothing worth defending.

But we're not left here to despair. The cross also makes sense of our life and its pain. In fact, what we did before Christ is nonsense and what we once considered absurd now makes complete sense. There is nothing in our life out of God's control. The therapeutic perspective can't get here. It can only patch us up and teach us how to walk with a limp. The gospel of sovereign grace transforms us and gives us new legs. It sets us free. All that happens to us—good and bad—presses us deep into the liberating reality of the mysterious cross. Our trials become messengers from God that teach us how to live with the rest of the sinners on this planet. Even our dads.

ALONE IS HARD TO TAKE

My biological father was a drummer in a rock band. My mom fell hard for him when she was really young. As a result, she never let me get near a drum set. (I think that qualifies as a "mommy wound.") They ran off together with Springsteen's "Born to Run" playing in the background of their naïveté. The joyride came to an end with the birth of their first child, my sister. It came off the rails with the birth of their second, me. As soon as my mom could raise enough money she left him to pursue his rock-and-roll fantasy. She was a mom now. That changed everything. He never grew up. Some things never change.

I was too young to know what had happened between them, or care. All I recall of my progenitor was an occasional visit in the summers of my youth. He was a cool customer and drove an even cooler custom van. Just imagine the seventies. He always had some beautiful woman with him who bore a striking resemblance to my mom. He would show up late morning to take my sister and me to lunch. The brief visit would end with a whirlwind trip to Kmart. With the brisk scent of materialism in my face he would confidently announce, "You can have anything you want, except a bike. That's too expensive." I settled for the Fonzie action figure with the movable thumb and miniature leather jacket. Then he would drop us off around three o'clock and leave. I had no idea who this guy was and why he bought me stuff. They told me he was my father, but that didn't make any sense. Weren't dads supposed to be around? Eventually, those outings came to an end.

I remember my mom being angry on the days he did come. That's about all I recall. Well, that and the fact that the arm of the Six Million Dollar Man action figure came off, revealing bionics. My mom would sit on the couch at my grandparents' home watching me play with my new little trinkets and weeping bitterly. She would eventually exit the room with a slam of the door. I would push my glasses up on my nose and stare curiously at the door through my cloudy little lenses. Adults were complicated. I was innocent and clueless. I imagine that's the only thing that saves a kid in my situation. Truly, for a five-year-old, ignorance is bliss, but short-lived.

I now know what it was about that scene that hurt her so deeply.

Me. There's nothing so sad as a boy without a father. It's like the emotion we have when we see people eating alone in restaurants. Alone is hard to take. Maybe the only thing more regrettable is the son whose father is present but might as well not be. Ultimately, both are alone in this world.

WHO DOESN'T WANT A FATHER?

Despite the absence of my biological father, I've avoided becoming a statistic. God, in His grace, sent me a replacement dad. Not long after my mom relocated she ran into a childhood friend of her brother's, Victor Yawn. Several years later—after they were married—I was sitting on a wooden bench outside a courtroom, legs swinging back and forth in thick Southern air. Victor came and stood across from me, then squatted so as to look me right in the eyes. He then asked, "Do you want to be my son?" A strange question for a kid who already assumed he was. I looked at him and said, "Yep." He disappeared into the courtroom. Later that day I was endowed with the worst last name a preacher could ever ask for, Yawn. A name for which I will forever be grateful.

That question is etched in my mind. It is a treasured memory. Imagine a day when the man who's already functioning as your dad makes it official by asking you the most obvious question on the planet. Who doesn't want a father? Believe me, I never took his presence for granted. In some ways I think there are a lot of men with biological children who need to get around to asking this same question. I'm pretty sure how their kids will answer. After all, who doesn't want a father?

Despite the fact I was adopted by him, I didn't realize he was my stepfather until many years later. For many it is the opposite scenario. Despite the fact that sons know who their biological fathers are, they don't actually *know* them. My dad's love was unconditional. This is why I have never referred to him as my stepfather, and bristle when others do. He never gave me a chance to know the difference. This only goes to prove the fact that many men who have kids aren't fathers at all.

Let's be clear. Any beast aroused at the right time with a suitable mate in view can produce an offspring. But only men can be fathers.

Furthermore, it's one thing for a father to be around; it's another thing for a father to be engaged. Obviously, being around is better than not being around, but being engaged is invaluable. One simply fills a role. The other anchors a life. It's obvious when a dad is merely tolerating his kid. No one knows this more than the kid. At the same time, nothing so enlivens the life of a child as a dad who cares. When dad is listening and tracking and caring for his son's soul, the world is a safer place.

It's unnatural for a father to ignore his children. It's cruel. It's a subtle form of abandonment. Kids are satisfied with the smallest crumb that occasionally falls from their father's table. Since most children get very little from their dads, they're content with whatever they get. Hence, "good, but not much." Dads can do the smallest things and effect enormous joy in their children. Just coming home from work is an event. Dads don't just come home. They arrive.

Most dads never notice the deep need for approval their sons carry around. It's potent. One word of encouragement can have a lifetime of effect. It only takes one sentence to change a son's life forever, "Son, I'm proud of you." Those men who've never received this type of approval spend a lifetime working for it. Those who get it have a sense of assurance the rest don't.

No dad is perfect. For the most part King David was a good father. Obviously he had some serious baggage, but he engaged with Solomon, warning his son to avoid the mistakes he made. Yet Solomon ended up the Casanova of the Bible. Then there was Saul—basically the Darth Vader of the Old Testament. Despite his stupidity he had an exemplary son like Jonathan. I guess the point is that so much is dependent on God's grace. You could be the best dad on the planet and still have a bonehead for a son. Or you could be a total failure and have a son who honors you despite your inability to be a father to him.

Some fathers are good at some things, but no father is good at everything. Some things we have to figure out on our own. Those who never had fathers, or had really poor ones, can take some comfort in this fact. Eventually, even those who had ideal relationships with their fathers find themselves in the tangle of their own lives, wishing their father had told them a little bit more.

A DAD TO THE END

Dr. Victor Yawn and my youngest sister were crossing over a long country road. She was taking him back to the ER. As I recall, he had been watching his granddaughter in a play. They looked both ways down the familiar expanse and then proceeded across. The car that hit them was hidden by a dip in the road. It was a freak accident. In the very moment they turned to see what was coming they could not see it. But, it was coming. When my sister awoke—having been knocked unconscious at impact—he was lying against his seat looking at her. He had been waiting for her. When their eyes met he asked, "Sweetheart, are you okay?" She said, "Yes, Daddy." He then closed his eyes, lay his head back, and surrendered to the internal injuries that eventually took his life. A dad to the end.

It was a bizarre phone call. "Your dad is not well; you should come home." I had listened to my dad make the same call to the families of his patients a hundred times. I knew what it meant. This agonizing awareness filled the six-hour ride home. A strange painful anticipation. I knew he was gone. It was the longest ride of my life. I collapsed in tears in the ER parking lot when I finally received the inevitable news.

When I encountered my mom some time later, she asked the most appropriate question I've ever heard: "What are we going to do without him?" There's only one answer to that question: "I don't know." Patriarchs are a tough loss. I've certainly not done as well as I would have otherwise.

Weeks before, my dad had been at my home in Dallas, Texas, where I was an associate pastor in a Bible church. We played golf, ate greasy food, contemplated life, annoyed our wives, and laughed. Father and son. He held my one-year-old daughter for a photo just before he departed. It hangs on the wall of my home.

In a sublime moment before his departure, which I will never forget, he took me around behind his Suburban. He looked me right in the eyes—no longer needing to squat down—and said, "Son, I'm so proud of you. I'm proud to call you my son. I just wanted you to know that." Then he left. I remember walking into the house after our encounter and telling my wife, Robin, "God just gave me a tremendous gift. Dad and I are no longer just father and son; we're friends. Best friends. I love that man." Two weeks later the phone rang.

What comforted me most in the days leading up to and following his funeral was the closure. It was all done. The last thing I ever said to my dad was, "I love you." We so often communicated our love to one another there was nothing I needed to say to him. As I've grown, however, there's plenty I wish he had said to me. I've faced a lot of questions where my impulse was to pick up the phone and call him. There's much more I wish he had said while he was still alive. Wisdom is a precious commodity. There's none so valuable and trustworthy as the wisdom of a father.

In a weird providence, I've been fatherless twice. This fact has caused me to know the value of male influences in my life. I've sought out these influences. I've asked thousands of questions. My dad died when I was twenty-seven. From there to here I have taken careful notes and paid close attention to good fathers and consistent men. I've listened.

I now have three sons of my own. One awaits me in heaven. The two remaining here on earth are affectionately known as "Hammer and Nail." Brothers. A fraternity I never had the privilege of experiencing. I love these boys. These boys love their dad. In many ways I'm a mooring for their lives. In others, they are a mooring for mine. Sons need dads in ways only being a dad makes obvious. All these principles I've picked up are now bombarding their world. Much of it is the content of this book.

I'm afraid for them. This world is brutal, especially for men. It's a grinder. So I try not to waste a moment. I give them every ounce of wisdom I have to give about everything I can imagine. This includes simple and mundane things. Why you should never cut into a steak to see if it's done. Why prevent defense never works. How you swing a hammer by holding it at the end of the handle. Then there are larger realities. Integrity. Love. Sex. Money. I never stop thinking about them and their future wives and kids. But mostly I pray. I know full well I'm a sinner raising sinners. Only God can do what needs to be done in their lives. I'm just an instrument.

The following chapters are some of what I want to say to my sons, as well as what I wish had been said to me. Principles. They come from various places. Some are hard-earned lessons. I've tried not to waste personal mistakes. As I have had the opportunity to do exit reviews on my blunders, various principles have emerged. My prayer is that what I've learned from my failures can preserve my sons from a similar fate. Other principles are borrowed from the wisdom of men in my life. I've made them my own over the years. They've been invaluable.

As you read, you'll notice gaps—things proved to be valuable in your own life that aren't included. This is inevitable. I've not intended to say *everything* that needed to be said, but only some of what every man wished he had known before. But as you compare notes with me, you should write down your thoughts. In fact, send me your suggestions, and I'll add them to my list. But, more importantly, get up and walk down the hall to your son's room, or pick up the phone to call your son. Tell him yourself. He's been waiting for this moment. Call your dad. Tell him you love him.

I know one day my sons will wish I had told them more than I did. This too is inevitable. Fact is, I can't tell them enough. So much will be up to them. As of now I'm trying—by God's grace—to give my sons the best head start in this life I can. So, I talk to them. I'm engaged. Every night I'm home to put them to bed, without fail I bury my face in theirs and say, "I love you, son. I'm proud to have you as a son." This isn't everything they need to hear, but if it were the last thing they heard from me, there'd be nothing left to say.

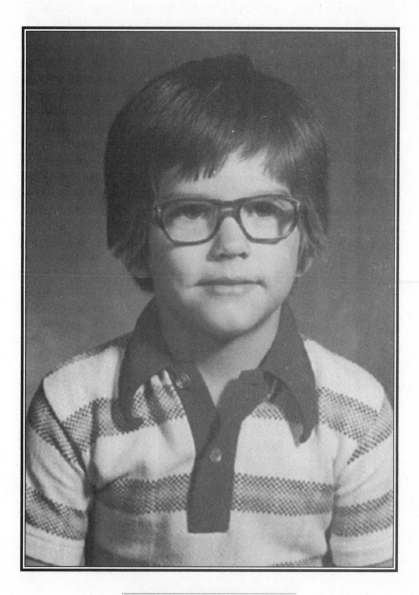

BYRON AT AGE FIVE

2

GRACE: NEVER MOVE
BEYOND THE GOSPEL

The word of the cross is foolishness to those who are perishing,
but to us who are being saved it is the power of God. For it is written,
"I will destroy the wisdom of the wise, and the cleverness of the clever
I will set aside." Where is the wise man? Where is the scribe? Where
is the debater of this age? Has not God made foolish the wisdom of
the world? For since in the wisdom of God the world through its
wisdom did not come to know God, God was well-pleased through
the foolishness of the message preached to save those who believe.
{ The apostle Paul, 1 Corinthians 1:18-21 }

There will come a time, as comes in everyone's life, when your progress is halted by the unwelcomed barnacles that attach themselves to our fallenness: marital strife, adultery, life-dominating sin, personal failure, an emotional breakdown, a rebellious child, a sick spouse, the tragic loss of a loved one, unconfessed sin, depression, anger, financial ruin, the ubiquitous test result for cancer that takes a brutal seven days to come back, etc. Everyone eventually gets to helplessness. In that moment, if you are like the rest of us, the last place you will turn will be to Jesus Christ. The gospel, streaming invisibly as a ticker across the bottom of your life, will seem powerless to affect the more "complex" issues of your existence. You will immediately assume your modern predicaments require more sophisticated solutions than the gospel. The gospel is comforting, but ineffective deep into the thick of life.

As you sit in the shadow of the unexpected you will be half insulted at the suggestion of the gospel's sufficiency. You will most likely turn away from the gospel, not toward it. I know this makes little sense, but it's usually true. Standing under your worst moments, the idea of turning to the gospel will appear as the naïve counsel of a caring grandmother. A veritable milk-and-cookies answer. The stuff of flannel boards and nursery rhymes. A vast oversimplification of your refined pain. "Christ and Him crucified" will appear as nothing more than a tattered cliché. Such is what men (even regenerate ones at times) have always said about the cross—*it is foolishness*.

THE SAME BAD ADVICE AS ALWAYS

Much of the wisdom we seek (or give ourselves) in our darkest moments is the same bad advice we've been giving ourselves since the dawn of time: Try harder. Maybe this is true because we're reluctant to admit the real root of our most exquisite aches—*sin*. It makes us feel better about ourselves to rely upon more advanced solutions. But all our specialized "Christian" wisdom, which courteously tips a hat to the gospel, ultimately ignores it and moves past it. It throws us back on our own strength and resources. Think deeper. Know more. Be better. Strive harder.

But this is the last thing fallen men need to hear, not the first. The cross says the exact opposite—*repent, rest, believe*. We give ourselves bad advice. If the cross proves anything, it is that man cannot lift the burden of sin and its consequences off of himself. If we were able, then Christ need not have died. He would have only needed to cheer us on. If the answer is to merely work harder, He died needlessly.

We drag our feet on the gospel because we have been taught to esteem it as the entry point of Christianity and not the totality of it. It gets us in, and then "we take it from there." We are ever grateful for the help it offered in getting us on our feet and through the pearly gates. We treat the gospel like the soldiers who gave their lives to secure our freedom. We stop to acknowledge their sacrifice on Memorial Day and then take our freedom for granted all the other days of the year. But we assume the gospel is a mere beginning. That we must believe it in order to be *saved* has come to imply that you need not believe it in order to *live*. But you are not only saved by grace, you are also *being saved* by it.

In our minds, our lives progress beyond the simple message of the gospel. Like getting past the need for training wheels, as we get better at life, the assistance they provided is no longer necessary. It becomes a reference point for progress. Like rings within a tree. "See how far we've come." In some strange way, we take "getting beyond the basics of the gospel" as a sign of personal improvement. But you never move beyond the gospel to a more sophisticated or timely wisdom. There is no more intricate or relevant wisdom than the cross. God has nothing more to offer. Its simplicity, which we take for granted, is also its complexity. It is not moved beyond. You don't get over it. You wade into its vastness. What should astound us is its ever-deepening and infinitely unfolding depth of wisdom. It is the marvel of the infinite mind of God.

Paul described himself as a steward of the gospel's immeasurable mysteries. He never got over it or moved past a dependence on it. He grew more basic in the sense that he was constantly coming to an awareness of the depth of those basic realities. His ever-growing need for it corresponded to his ever-increasing awareness of its enormity. He saw it. It consumed him. It was like digging through silos of unending grain. The deeper he dug, the deeper he dug. As he turned it over, it grew more glorious, not less. With each examination it grew more substantial, not less. It became more relevant, not less. If you see it, you bow before it. You do not scoot around it. Its circumference is infinite.

It is hard for those of us who have been saved by the gospel's power to remember that we live by it also. Tracing our life's circumstance up to the foot of the cross is hard. We don't easily see the gospel's relevance, or how it applies to the everyday things, much less the thorny ones. But if you should ever go from "hearing" to "seeing," you will behold the truth. The gospel comes down like a heads-up display of clarity in our life. It makes life make sense. It is the "wisdom of God." As such, we discover over and over how it matches perfectly with our hard heads, broken hearts, and bent knees.

The cross is a counterintuitive reality. It rebuffs nearly all the world's wisdom and our expertise at every point. Normally, whatever your heart counsels you to do, you'd be well advised to do the exact opposite. We say live. The cross says die. We say defend. The cross says lay down. We say power. The cross says humility. We say vengeance. The cross says forgiveness. We say indulgence. The cross says moderation.

We say self. The cross says service. We say us. The cross says others. We say happiness. The cross says holiness. We say try harder. The cross says repent of trying. This explains the very reason we have such a hard time beholding the gospel's relevance.

I SAW WHAT THEY SAW

I was milling about my house one Wednesday night around the age of sixteen. I was a poster child for the arrogant and confused adolescent male. My parents—who had recently "found religion" and were making my life more miserable than usual—were at a prayer meeting with some old people. I thought they had gone crazy. They went so far as to throw my Lynyrd Skynyrd CDs in the trash. They inundated me with Bible-speak about life and death and Jesus. I didn't really understand it. What I did understand was that they desperately wanted me to understand it. But I could not see it. There were many tear-filled appeals.

That night alone in my house, in a moment, as if my eyes were suddenly opened, what my parents had been saying to me for months made sense. I saw it. It was clear to me. When you finally see your sin, the cross always makes perfect sense. The gospel opens up to us as the complete summary of all God is. I fell on my face and cried out for God's mercy. The cross was the only logical solution to my real problem. I knew this was what my parents had been telling me.

I had grown up in a denomination that featured altar calls. That's all I remembered about "church" at the time. So I did what I thought I was supposed to do. I drove (very carefully) to the church where my parents were praying—for their son's soul. I slipped in the back and waited until the prayer meeting—populated by twenty or so gray heads and my parents—was over. When it ended I went forward. I walked straight up (the aisle) to the pastor and said, "I need to be saved." He looked straight back at me and replied, "You don't need to be. You have been." He knew then what I know now. Only "those who are being saved" see it.

What else except the sovereign grace of God would cause me to admit my need for the cross? I freely admitted what my parents had tried to convince me of—*I was a sinner*. My parents' reaction? They were frozen—all but the flow of tears spilling out of their hearts—with hands over open mouths. (This prayer thing was powerful.) They knew I had seen what they saw. You can see it on the faces of those who finally behold it.

And I kept seeing it. Things that were impossibly difficult for me to swallow, like apologizing to my parents, made complete sense to me now. I actually realized the power and freedom in admitting my failures to them. The cross made even that make sense. Whereas I disrespected them at every turn before, I was now compelled to please them for no other reason than the freedom to do so. It brought me pleasure to throw my former way of life under the bus. It was an odd type of liberation. An unloading of my treachery.

I saw many other realities that I had been blind to. Foremost was the blessing of my father. I had been so disrespectful to him. He had loved me unconditionally as his own son, and I had spurned him like an enemy. I started the habit of getting out of bed around 5:30 a.m. during the weekdays to join him in prayer downstairs. Half the time, as his head was bowed, I'd be looking at him marveling and weeping. I saw God's grace toward me in this man. I regretted how rebellious I had been. From this side of the cross, my sin was appalling. Often, when he would finish praying, I would reach out for him and say, "Dad, I'm so sorry for how I've lived. Please forgive me." "Son," he would reply, "You are forgiven. You don't have to keep saying that." I knew this, but saying it made sense.

What Only the Gospel Can Do

In the light of the gospel, we can see the truth in what had previously made no sense at all. As someone once said, grace slips in and changes all the price tags in the display window. Everything is new. We see life through the lens of eternity and the Savior's love.

This perspective is especially powerful given my role as a pastor. When the insanity of adultery sits in front of me, I see more than an unthinking idiot and a broken family. I see a corrupt heart that has been so deceived by the idolatry of self it will sacrifice the most sacred realities of life in order to serve its demands. Only the gospel will usher us past the hatred and confusion to this truth. Only the cross will appear as the real solution to such deep confusion and sin. It tells the adulterer what's truly wrong and the broken spouse how forgiveness is even possible.

Every other wisdom stops short of it and fumbles around with symptoms lying around on the surface. Grace makes a family out of a disaster.

The gospel gets to the root. It takes this man's selfishness and transforms it into sacrifice. He now understands the power in servant-leadership and sacrificial love toward his bride. No longer is the aim finding a woman who can make him happy, but finding a woman to serve and love in the spirit of Christ's own sacrifice. As C.H. Spurgeon said, "His repentance becomes more notorious than his sin."

When the agony of a promiscuous young lady weeps in front of me, I don't see a statistic, or damaged goods. I see a sinful heart that has tried to fill itself with and find its worth in the affection of other human beings. Another empty idolatry made worse by the constant deception of the culture. The gospel reminds us that we have been freed from the tyranny of self. It is a love that loves unconditionally. It turns this heart back to that which it was designed to love—God. It makes a faithful wife out of a harlot.

One glance at the cross and we immediately know the problem is much deeper than our superficial answers. The gospel turns all our wisdom on its ear. The cross becomes wisdom and makes us look foolish. We suggest self-esteem as the solution to man's poor condition. The cross prescribes self-sacrifice. We offer moralism as the remedy for behavioral problems. The gospel offers grace. What we call an addiction the cross calls slavery. Our standard of measurement is relative. The cross's is absolute righteousness. We will always get it backward. We would never think to suggest what the gospel has been saying all along. The gospel knows. It has always known.

You cannot step into manhood without the gospel leading the way. The reason so many men struggle is because they have not stepped aside and let it. The mountain of responsibility is too steep to make it on your own. You can't make it by reaching for your bootstraps. You make it by bowing to the strength of another.

Without the gospel, we're in trouble. When we fail to live up to our own expectations, we'll despair. When we fail to live up to the expectations of others, we'll become resentful. When we fail to live up to our wife's expectations, we'll become angry. The gospel rescues us from despair, resentment, and anger. It frees us from performance and binds us to freedom. We don't have to be perfect men. There was only one of those. We have to be broken ones.

The gospel is a dad's only hope. It allows me to get past "lines and lists" in the raising of my children and speak right to the issues underlying their struggles. The gospel clearly says that every person's (including your children's) greatest need lies beneath moral conformity, or the lack thereof. Parenting is about addressing heart issues. Only the power of God through the gospel has the power to change your children's hearts. If it were otherwise, we would despair as we faced a responsibility we are powerless to fulfill. We would collapse under the weight of a reality only God can bear. We would treat symptoms and not root causes. We would simply throw the sanitizing effect of morality over the surface of our children's lives when purification at the root is what they need. We will frustrate them as much as we are frustrated by them, as we put a yoke on them that not even we can bear.

But the gospel gets down to specifics in parenting. It can handle the nitty gritty. When my sons deal with matters of sexuality or the opposite sex, the cross is there to clarify. It alone can teach them how self-sacrifice offers the power to resist immorality in the former and is the motivation for servant-leadership in the latter. I believe if my sons adore Jesus Christ and exalt Him as the exclusive object of worship in their lives, they will gladly lay down their lives in each case. The suffering of our Savior gives our obedience meaning. His resurrection gives it power. The Holy Spirit can teach my sons lessons I could never hope to teach. The gospel can carry them much farther than I could ever hope to. Jesus is that great.

Consider the apostle Paul in his letter to believers in Ephesus. He could have prayed for many things. No doubt there were interpersonal conflicts. No doubt there were financial issues. No doubt there were individual crises. Hurting people. Struggles. After all, it's the church. Here's what he prayed,

> For this reason I bow my knees before the Father, from whom every family in heaven and on earth derives its name, that He would grant you, according to the riches of His glory, to be strengthened with power through His Spirit in the inner man; so that Christ may dwell in your hearts

through faith; and that you, being rooted and grounded in love, may be able to comprehend with all the saints what is the breadth and length and height and depth, and to know the love of Christ which surpasses knowledge, that you may be filled up to all the fullness of God.

Now to Him who is able to do far more abundantly beyond all that we ask or think, according to the power that works within us, to Him be the glory in the church and in Christ Jesus to all generations forever and ever. Amen (Ephesians 3:14-21).

In so praying, Paul prayed for every one of those potential realities as he asked that the gospel and the glory of the cross would become real to the Ephesians on levels they had never deemed possible. He knew that the gospel—in all of its infinite mysteries—could do that which needed to be done in the hearts and lives of the people.

This is true of marriage as well. What compels me to love my wife as I should is not the performance of my spouse but the love of God toward me in Christ, which is powerful enough to carry me beyond her failure to love me perfectly. When I want to serve myself, the gospel and Christ compel me to do otherwise. I can let go of the need to serve myself at her expense simply because my Savior did so in love toward me. His love compels me to do the same.

We move beyond the gospel to our own demise. There will be barnacles. Life is not easy. Sin makes certain of this. It is hard. One day you will hold your wife in your arms in sight of a tragedy. She will turn to you for an explanation. In my case it was two precious babies (twins Zachary and Madeline) who had not lived but a few moments after birth. What do you say in the face of such pain? Nothing. Clever sound bites will be foolish nonsense to the mother of deceased children. I put my hand over my mouth and let God speak. I pointed to an empty tomb. The hole blown through death's prison by Christ's sacrifice and resurrection. I pointed to the only thing that would make it make sense. The gospel.

3

Masculinity:
Manhood Is Knowing
Where the Plunger Is

*When He had washed their feet, and taken His garments and
reclined at the table again, He said to them, "Do you know what
I have done to you? You call Me Teacher and Lord; and you are
right, for so I am. If I then, the Lord and the Teacher, washed
your feet, you also ought to wash one another's feet. For I gave
you an example that you also should do as I did to you."*

{ John 13:12-15 }

emember that scene in *Bourne Identity* when Jason and Marie
are holed up at Eamon's country home outside Paris? (Man Law
Alert: Never admit you've never seen the Bourne series.) Marie wakes
up in the night to find Jason standing over the children's bed. Assassin
now protector in repose regretting past assignments. A bit of foreshad-
owing, no doubt. A whispered discussion about simplicity and escaping to domestic realities ensues. Marie hesitates. The wandering gypsy
is as lonely as Jason. Will the two souls ever find each other? Such irony.
It's deep stuff. Okay, let's get back to explosions and gunfire.

Next morning the missing dog signals danger. Not like Lassie, mind
you. The dog is missing and this fact actually alerts Jason to danger. A
missing dog could not alert someone to danger because it's missing.
Anyway. Eamon and the children flee to the basement on Jason's com-
mand. Jason instinctually finds the shotgun above the hutch.

In her panic Marie says something like, "We've endangered the children!" Bourne, with ice in his veins, replies...wait for it..."That's not going to happen." And there it is. Man, I love that scene! At that moment I always wish Jason Bourne were my dad, or had come by my house for breakfast when I was eight. I go around my house quoting that phrase in Bourne-like inflection about everything—purchases, requests to play outside, sleepovers, or whatever. I usually end up saying yes, but it's so fun. My kids roll their eyes.

WHERE'S THE PLUNGER?

Okay, let's push back from fantasy for a moment (keep in mind I own the trilogy and can quote the movies verbatim) and pose a question. Who is the real hero here? Is it the Treadstone agent who—despite the numbers of assassins, bullets, wrecks, or falls—won't die? In Ludlum's depiction, yes, but not in reality. In reality, the real hero is Eamon. The frumpy figure way in Bourne's background sitting in his robe drinking the morning's coffee. The average dad. Eamon was no doubt intended to be a foil against the masculinity of Bourne. But I see it the other way around. Sure, Bourne can find the gun, but does he know where the plunger is? Besides, Eamon was man enough to care for his two young children and dog while his wife was away. Would you leave your kids with Bourne? I think not.

When Eamon realizes how Bourne irresponsibly drew his children and entire family into danger, he instinctually goes into lecture mode. Who has the nerve to lecture Jason Bourne? A dad. Dads are deadly at impromptu homilies on misbehavior. Clearly, Eamon is the only adult in the house. You can stand over children and romanticize about them all day, but this is meaningless. Come talk to me when you have to put down your weapon and change their poopie diapers. What's more frightening? A lurking assassin, or a toddler's mess?

Think about it. In a few days Eamon will have to pay for the propane tank Bourne incinerated saving his own skin. He'll have to repair the door-facing Jason kicked in as he entered his house illegally. He'll be retained for questioning by police. After all, his gun was used in the murder of a mysterious man now lying in a field. He'll pay hundreds of dollars in therapy for his children due to posttraumatic stress. He'll have to face the most necessary evil known to men, the Homeowners Association. And just wait until his wife gets home. Can you imagine the look on her face? He'll have to explain how he knows Marie.

It's astonishing how many books written on "biblical" masculinity make us feel ashamed of Eamon. Not so subtly, routine obligations and ordinary tasks lose their "pop." We resist "ordinary" like the plague. Many Christian books on masculinity intentionally irritate some "unfulfilled potential" in our souls. It "must be reached" to be real men. We must break free of Eamon's ordinariness to be the men we can be. We must answer that pesky primal call we've been unable to put our fingers on. It's our inner Jason Bourne calling out to us. We must protect, defend, etc. Such is the appeal. But these descriptions of masculinity are often counterproductive. In many instances, they give already irresponsible men a motivation for more irresponsibility. "Let's go kick a door off its hinges!"

It's all highly romanticized, especially the depictions in Christian books. Much of it has nothing to do with biblical manhood or reality. What if Eamon is a quadriplegic and can't jump off rocks? What if his wife has Alzheimer's? What if he works in a mailroom? What if he doesn't possess a spirit for adventure, but Scrabble? What if he doesn't like camping? What if he doesn't own a gun? (Man Law Alert: Never admit you don't own a gun.) What if the toilet is clogged?

If the biblical manhood we offer has no application to the ordinary, or reality, it isn't. I think we may have overreacted to the emasculation going on in our culture. We've exchanged one stereotype (men are universal idiots) for another one (the Marlboro man).

JESUS CRASHES OUR BARBECUE

If we mean to put forth definitions and examples of biblical manhood, shouldn't we look to Jesus Christ? Of course we should. Jesus was the perfect man. He *is* biblical masculinity. Yet our Lord is rarely put forth as the prototype—even in Christian responses. We look to biblical figures like Moses, Elijah or Boaz, but all these men point to Jesus. Or we look to historic figures known for various virtues, but many of these men didn't even know Jesus. Jesus is greater than both.

Many insightful people have pointed out the challenges to masculinity coming at us from certain quarters—the cultural neutering of the American male, androgynous Christianity, the pervasive contempt for masculinity in all things, etc. The world mocks Eamon. I get it. We don't have to go around apologizing for being men. Man up! Campfires. Knives. Bacon. Ten knots every man should know. No argument there.

I'm grateful for all those who are willing to say it. But many who have warned against the feminization of men in the church have also failed to present an *actual* biblical remedy. For certain Jesus didn't wear a skirt, but He didn't brandish a Desert Eagle XIX either (pretend you know what that is). Point is, either Jesus suffers from such overstatement that He ends up seeming more like Jack Bauer (moment of silence, please), or He's never mentioned. I'm afraid in the end our response looks a little...well...childish.

It's not William Wallace we should emulate, but Jesus Christ. Only He can transform weak men into real ones and boys into men. Honestly, I think we avoid Jesus because He conflicts with our preferences. Even Jesus doesn't live up to the popular Christian vision of manhood—and He founded Christianity.

When you look to Christ you are beholding real strength, fortitude, character, determination, zeal, conviction, endurance, and courage. But, like all things Christ, it's counterintuitive. It does not come out in bravado, but humility. True strength is found in restraint, and not dominance. Fortitude is seen in quiet suffering, and not hardheadedness. Character is visible in consistency, and not status. Determination is evident in patience, and not headstrong belligerence. Real zeal is aimed toward God, and not found in self-determination. Real power is doing what you should, instead of what you'd rather. What we'd rather do is usually easier. In a word, strength is *restraint*.

If Jesus is what it means to be a man, then any biblical definition of manhood will of necessity have a cross in it. The cross and Jesus are synonymous. At the center of biblical masculinity is the cross of Christ and the sacrifice that comes with it. The absence of sacrifice is where popular versions of masculinity coming from the church fail to capture the reality.

According to Isaiah, Jesus was so ordinary as to go unnoticed. He was a humble carpenter. About as typical an occupation as one could find. The ancient equivalent of a computer analyst. Jesus was punched in the face and did not retaliate with an amazing bicycle kick to the back of the head. He was verbally assaulted and never crushed His opponents with laser beam-like sarcastic comebacks. When they spit in His face He didn't go ballistic and defend His honor. When He was wrongly accused He never stood up for Himself with devastating argumentation. He would have known where the shotgun was (for He is omniscient), but He would not have used it. How's that for male bravado? We'd never invite Jesus to our barbecue. Which is Isaiah's point.

HOW TO USE A BASIN IN ONE EASY STEP

Jesus cautioned His apostles against the tendency toward romanticized visions of masculinity and authority. The very same ones we suffer from. He did not promote power and self-assertiveness, but humility and service to others. He was not about those things. As the disciples journeyed with Jesus for three years, He spent more time rending this stereotype from their minds than any other. Incessantly, He taught them what it meant to be a man in His kingdom.

> Jesus called them to Himself, and said, "You know that the rulers of the Gentiles lord it over them, and their great men exercise authority over them. It is not this way among you, but whoever wishes to become great among you shall be your servant, and whoever wishes to be first among you shall be your slave; just as the Son of Man did not come to be served, but to serve, and to give His life a ransom for many" (Matthew 20:25-28).

While the disciples debated over who would sit nearest the front at Jesus' inauguration, Jesus encouraged them to give up their seats.

While they volleyed for spots in His cabinet, He demonstrated how to use a servant's basin. They even argued about prominence and power on the very evening He was arrested. That image of Jesus, the maker of heaven and earth, on His knees like a commonplace servant washing the disciples' feet is the most complete image of manhood known to us.

> Jesus, knowing that the Father had given all things into His hands, and that He had come forth from God, and was going back to God, got up from supper, and laid aside His garments; and taking a towel, He girded Himself. Then He poured water into the basin, and began to wash the disciples' feet, and to wipe them with the towel with which He was girded (John 13:3-5).

Biblical manhood is servant leadership.

Look, I know Jesus got after the temple market with a cat-o'-nine-tails. Twice. It must have been awesome to watch. But don't extrapolate from that the version of biblical masculinity you'd like to see adopted. It's not what you think. He was righteously indignant about the commercialization of the sacrificial system. The essence of worship had been corrupted. In so doing, Jesus put a bull's eye on His back. He stood alone. It would be the same if you were to stand up in church one Sunday—in the middle of a sermon—and take your pastor to task because he hedged on the gospel for the sake of pragmatism. What? Not willing to go that far for the truth? Coward.

THE MEN THE HEROES
DEPEND ON ARE MY HEROES

Biblical manhood is not hard to grasp. The men we're looking for are humble, quiet, and faithful in little. They are there like Eamon, sitting in the background of all our fiction. They possess all those virtues that make the rest of us seem immature and selfish: self-discipline, foresight, stability, security, and consistency. They are dependable. (What a devastating word for the majority of men!) I find them extraordinary and rare. There's no flash or bang, but there is consistency.

They're the type of men the rest of us depend on. They require little prompting in their role. They see the importance of balancing the checkbook, paying bills (on time), mowing the yard (every week), changing the oil (every 3000 miles). They know where the plunger is and aren't afraid to use it. They're husbands and dads. My heroes are the normal guys who do normal things well. Not normal men who do (cliché dead ahead) extraordinary things.

Many men look at the "monotony" of domestic realities and yearn for more dramatic ones. Such is the reason so many men abandon their wives and families for more impressive and exhilarating contexts. Such is the reason husbands and fathers get bored with wives and children and retreat to complacency. They're self-absorbed, not sacrificial. The church constantly contributes to this attitude. Our primary concern seems to be the progress of their self-discovery. While it is important to be comfortable in your own skin as a man and not be ashamed of masculinity, these mind-sets merely complement the nature of biblical manhood. They don't define it.

This is why the cross of Jesus is so central to manhood. It is the only truth that makes the ordinary experiences of husbands and fathers the most exhilarating adventure we can know. We're servants, not spies. The potential for obscurity as you sacrifice yourself for others takes far more courage than self-realization. What keeps us to our duty with robust passion is the image of Christ on His knees serving us.

It's the simple things. Like when I carry my sleeping child to bed— his sweaty little mane of hair resting on my shoulder. He needs me to do that. But, behind that and a thousand other transports is a greater reality. His entire life leans on mine. I am moved by that truth like none other. I love my children desperately. What a magnificent and weighty responsibility this reality is. I love it so.

Manhood is my wife and me balled up on the floor weeping at the loss of our twins. Same shoulder, different distance to traverse. Her brokenness is held together by my compassion. This is real stuff, not fantasy. It's not sexy like a knife duel, but it requires far more strength and is far more thrilling to the heart of a real man.

Muriel McQuilkin, wife of Robertson, former president of

Columbia International University, was diagnosed with Alzheimer's disease at the zenith of her husband's career. Alzheimer's, the "slow darkness," overtakes its victims with an ever-increasing dementia until the person vanishes behind the tangle of a confused mind. This disease is way too prevalent among our elderly.

Part of the loss is not only the slow physical death of a person, but also the incremental destruction of that person's dignity. Unless you've been there, you'll never know how hard it is to stare into the terrified eyes of a mother or father who suddenly forgets how to open a door. Out of an effort to honor their parents, adult children usually rally around their parent's dignity and protect it as they watch them disappear into the confusion.

In the beginning, Robertson was able to juggle his responsibilities as a caregiving husband and president of a thriving institution. Before long, however, it was no longer possible to be adequate at both. In the intervening days he wrestled with the inevitable decision—institutionalization, or not? A powerful image appeared in his mind:

> Would anyone love her at all, let alone love her as I do? I
> had often seen the empty, listless faces of those lined up
> in wheelchairs along the corridors of such places waiting,
> waiting for the fleeting visit of some loved one.[1]

Eventually Robertson resigned his post as president to take up his basin as servant (husband). He walked away from prominence and influence for a posture of servitude.

Many people assumed the decision would have been regretful on some levels. After all, he gave so much away. When answering this sort of query about his decision his answer was always the same: "She is such a delight to me. I don't have to care for her, I get to." And at that, the angels in heaven rise in applause. It's awe-inspiring when we men get it right.

Such is real courage.

WADE AND BLAKE ✕ AGES FOUR AND TWO

4

AFFECTION:
"I LOVE YOU, SON"

*What man is there among you who, when his son asks for a
loaf, will give him a stone? Or if he asks for a fish, he will not
give him a snake, will he? If you then, being evil, know how to
give good gifts to your children, how much more will your Father
who is in heaven give what is good to those who ask Him!*

{ MATTHEW 7:9-11 }

T he late Tim Russert's *Big Russ and Me*, which chronicled his
relationship with his father, was and remains an extremely popular work. One reviewer described the book as "*The Greatest Generation* meets *Tuesdays with Morrie*." At the time of its publication it
touched a nerve in adult children all over the country, especially sons.
People from all types of backgrounds simultaneously related to Russert's descriptions of his dad. It resonated. He unwittingly wrote for
generations of adult children, capturing in written words the unspoken
feelings and emotions that resided deep in their own hearts.

Russert received nearly 60,000 letters and e-mails in response. This
palpable reaction surprised him. (And then again it isn't very surprising.) Those who wrote were compelled to share some element of their
relationship with their own father. It was as if they needed to memorialize their respect for the man who gave them life. Prior to his death
Russert compiled those letters in a follow-up book, *Wisdom of Our
Fathers*. It too is a very encouraging read. In the introduction he wrote,

> Luke, Maureen, and I always go to Buffalo for Thanksgiv-
> ing, and in 2004, a few months after the book came out,
> we were loading up the car to head to the airport when

Big Russ came over to me to say good-bye. For as long as I can remember, Dad and I always parted with a handshake and a half hug. But this time he gave me a huge bear hug and said softly, "I love you"—something I had never heard before. I was fifty-four years old, and all I could think was, Boy, I wish I had written this book thirty years earlier.[2]

In all honesty, I was disappointed at this revelation. Fifty-four years old and he never heard his father say, "I love you." One would naturally have assumed otherwise given the obvious bond that existed between father and son. Two books were dedicated to his relationship with his father. This makes little sense to me. In my mind only pride can keep a father from telling his son he loves him. Characterize it as simplicity or stoicism, but it's still pride.

"My dad didn't need to tell me he loved me. He showed me. He provided for me every day." This is a common excuse for those who never heard their fathers express their love verbally. Obviously, providing for one's family is commendable. Making sure your kids have everything they need is biblical. It is a part of love. But to suggest a father expressing his love to his children is nonessential is ridiculous. "He did not need to" still implies that he should have. As is obvious in Russert's case, it was long overdue.

Ask any grown man if he regrets never having heard his dad express his love for him and he will probably tell you no. But of course he regrets it. All you need to do is change the question, "Would you have preferred it?" The answer is always yes. This is due to an obvious principle. You're supposed to tell the people you love that you love them. Expressing affection is part of our makeup as human beings. Some men may see it as weakness, but this way of thinking is attached to a wrong understanding of masculinity. Biblical masculinity includes passion.

REALLY BAD GIRLFRIENDS

Men are constantly criticized (by women) for not being emotional. As you've no doubt heard, we're not "in touch with our emotions." This is a chief criticism from wives. They're concerned (frustrated) that their husbands don't (or won't) express their feelings. According to them, it hinders the marriage. I hear it all the time. "Jim has a hard time talking about his feelings. He won't open up." They pry at their husbands' emotions like they're opening a can of peas. In response, their husbands go inward. It's somewhat of a predictable cycle. What I wish I could say is this: "Lady, if Jim could get a word in he'd tell you exactly how he 'feels.' He 'feels' very well and is never going to be a woman."

What many wives actually want—without realizing it—is for "Jim" to be more like a girlfriend than a husband. (Unfortunately, some men would make good women. But that's another chapter.) Some women expect their men to have the same range of emotions and sensitivities as they do. On a much broader scale, it's generally assumed within the culture that the world would be a better place if men were more like women. There's no way this would be a good thing. The differences are God-ordained. We depend on these differences as a race. They are essential to the roles of husbands and wives. Bottom line—husbands aren't girlfriends and aren't supposed to be.

I admit that women are more expressive of their emotions, but this does not mean men don't feel. I feel all kinds of emotions as a man. I didn't cry at *Fried Green Tomatoes* like a buddy of mine, but I feel nonetheless. Like most men, I don't go around telling everyone about my feelings. Why should I? More often than not it's counterproductive to my role as a leader. Who wants to be led by someone who gives over common sense and reacts emotionally to every situation? I've been under this type of leadership. It's utterly frustrating.

What does being in touch with your emotions really mean anyway? As best I can tell, it's the ability and freedom to express or describe one's "inner child." Basically, talking about how you feel. Removing the filter of discretion and letting it flow. If I'm angry, I tell you. If I'm sad and don't know why, buckle up. You're about to be my therapist for the next thirty minutes. "Good, Jim! Good! Let it out." But is it really healthy or productive to tell anyone who will listen everything you're feeling every time you feel something? No. It's unhealthy, not to mention annoying.

To be in touch with your emotions does not mean you should live according to them. People who do are usually basket cases. Emotions are untrustworthy guides. Nor does being emotional mean you have to express what you feel in every situation. Usually people need time to process their emotions by comparing them to reality so as to determine the appropriate reaction. Telling people what you're thinking all the time can do more harm than good. This is especially true in the midst of a crisis or disagreement.

IT'S A HEADS-UP DISPLAY

On the other hand, I know where this criticism comes from and at what it's aimed. On some levels it's a valid complaint. Husbands and fathers who are emotionally unavailable put those under their care at an enormous disadvantage. This is inevitable. If the individual responsible for providing guidance remains silent, it can only result in frustration for those who depend upon him. When a dad doesn't express matters of approval or disapproval, encouragement or disappointment, his children may wander in confusion. This is the very reason many daughters who did not receive any attention from their fathers make messes of their lives seeking it from other men later in life.

Kids depend upon dad to help define right and wrong actions, good and bad attitudes. It's part of being a leader. The encouragement and discipline that come from a dad are invaluable. It's a heads-up display of principles that last a lifetime, guiding kids through all sorts of circumstances. When a dad refuses to open up and tell his children how he feels about them, it robs them of this essential ingredient in their development.

Fact is, sons yearn for their dad's approval (or disapproval). It puts a certain structure around their lives that can come from nothing else. The encouragement or correction they receive sticks with them for a lifetime. Sons naturally trust their dad's counsel. As they progress into adulthood those little lessons and insights that come from moments of loving and affectionate instruction continue to guide them. This is why men whose fathers took the time to express their feelings seem to have a greater level of confidence. They've always known where they stood.

Above all else, sons need to know their fathers love them. Every son needs to hear his dad say, "I love you." It's not really optional. This is especially true when it's hardest to say—when their sons fail or disappoint. Life is hard and fraught with painful mistakes. My sons need to understand that this is a normal part of life. More importantly, they need to know that my love for them is not contingent upon their pleasing me at all times. They need to get a glimpse of God's grace in my reaction to their most substantial struggles.

The expression of love I have in mind is not just the verbalization of three specific words but also a tone and volume in the father's voice and heart. It's the sound of encouragement when a son is struggling to figure something out. It's the sweetness of forgiveness after failure and discipline. It's a levelheaded correction instead of an outburst of anger. It's an uplifting moment of guidance instead of a biting condescension. It's the resonance of respect when they reach a certain age. It's the balance of patience after the fiftieth question. Collectively it all communicates love.

As a father of sons, I know what it is to struggle with their shortcomings. Boys are still banging rocks long after girls begin to grow up. I want my sons to mature and grow so badly sometimes I don't give them time to do it. I can get frustrated with the impulsive things boys are prone to do. When my frustration shows it greatly affects them. They carry a heavy burden around—a burden that creates an uncertainty. Unfortunately, if my love for them has not been made obvious, our relationship may appear to be conditioned upon their performance. This is the exact opposite of the message of Christ: "God demonstrates His own love toward us, in that while we were yet sinners, Christ died for us" (Romans 5:8).

What my sons need to know, especially at these moments, is that their dad loves them regardless. It's a way of communicating the unconditional love of God in the cross. This type of love sets them free to overcome their struggles. Knowing they'll never be rejected by me even when they blow it allows them to recover, learn, correct, and move on. I'm not speaking of a permissiveness that ignores their misbehavior. That type of parenting is destructive, not helpful. What I'm referring to is a love that is evident even when correction is called for. Or a type of correction that has love as a characteristic. It's always there picking them up when they fall, lifting them up when they're down, and holding them up when they struggle.

Before becoming engaged to my wife I faced some important decisions about school and work. I wrestled with the options for a couple of days and then finally approached my dad and sought his counsel. I remember sitting opposite him at our breakfast room table and laying it all out. I'm sure it was all ordinary stuff to him, but he had this way of making you think it was the most important consideration of his day. We prayed and that was that. I went off to bed.

The next morning there was a note from my dad on the kitchen counter scribbled on a notepad with some pharmaceutical company's logo on it. My dad's penmanship was a joke. It was like hieroglyphics. He wrote everything in the same handwriting he used to write prescriptions. There were only a few people on the planet who could decipher it—his wife, nurse, and children. I'm not even sure he could make it out.

That's been twenty years ago now. I still have that note. It's a worthless scrap of paper to anyone else, but it's a treasure to me. The fact he took the time to write it was encouraging beyond description. No doubt he had no idea how much it meant to me at the time. Which is usually the case with dads and their sons. It's the small things. His note read,

> Boo
>
> I will be praying for you and your decision at work.
> I will support you whatever you decide.
>
> In Christ
> Dad

Not every son has one of these. But every son should.

5

AMBITION: NEVER CHOOSE NOT TO SUCCEED

Hear, my son, and accept my sayings and the years of your life will be many. I have directed you in the way of wisdom; I have led you in upright paths. When you walk, your steps will not be impeded; and if you run, you will not stumble. Take hold of instruction; do not let go. Guard her, for she is your life.

{ PROVERBS 4:10-13 }

A s I've provided counsel for young men over the years on everything from marriage to finances, I've come to realize one fact: There's no end to the advice they'll need. The world ahead of them is fraught with significant decisions. It comes at them fast. One day they can't keep up with their retainers. The next they have kids. Much of what I provide by way of counsel is not complicated stuff. It's basic. "Don't cut into a steak to see if it's done." Fact is, this information should have been distributed by their fathers years before. So much could have been accomplished by simple little conversations. Teachable moments. That's what dads are supposed to do. The void is regrettable and unnecessary.

As these naïve creatures start the rapid ascent toward maturity, the heaviness of responsibility piles up in the form of choices. Xbox or PS3? Kirk or Picard? Which college should I choose? What degree should I pursue? Which career path should I take? Should I stay on my current course? How do I know if I should get married right now? How do I know if she's the one? When should we have kids? They roll out of bed

one day (around noon) to face the starkness of reality—life is complicated. It doesn't help matters that they've spent their first two decades
ignoring anything resembling maturity.

ONE HARD DECISION AFTER ANOTHER

Basically, becoming a man is one hard decision after another. It's accu-
mulative. Fundamentally, good decision-making is a learned skill.
More often than not, the ability to make good decisions is the result of
making bad ones first. Every successful man has committed a blunder
or two along the way. Bolstered by enthusiasm or blinded by impul-
siveness, they strike out in the wrong direction. Or they head out in the
right direction with the wrong approach. It happens. How one reacts
to bad decisions made is often more important than having made a
good one. An insightful man once said, "It's a wise man who makes a
good second decision." But decisions have to be made.

Hundreds of counseling sessions later, clearly discernible patterns
have appeared. Various responsibilities loom within certain stages of
life. Men go through very predictable seasons of decisions in their mat-
uration process. Although these "miniature" crises seem insurmount-
able to them at the time (the proverbial mountain out of a molehill),
they're actually pretty standard. As young men schedule time with me
I can almost predict the category of life issue we'll be discussing.

All of life's unavoidable thresholds present unique challenges and
decisions. It's part of life. But this predictability is good news. For one,
it means the pressure they feel is normal. "You're not crazy" is good for
anxious young men to hear. Nearly every man has experienced similar
challenges at some point in his life. It also means there's wisdom available. Other men have faced tough decisions and lived to tell about it.
They only need to ask.

Despite the available clarity, many young men find themselves para-
lyzed by fear and analysis. Even with encouragement and counsel many
remain indecisive. Often for decades. Others simply push aside their
responsibility for as long as they can, succumbing to their bent toward
apathy. Boredom, it turns out, is a very underestimated emotion.

Personally, there may be no more frustrating individual than the immature and unmotivated adolescent male. They pang me. Barely good for growing hair and producing carbon dioxide. It's a waste of life. When they should be thriving they're donning wireless headsets in their mother's basement challenging some eight-year-old in Arizona at Halo.

DECIDING NOT TO DECIDE IS A DECISION

Lately, however, as I've walked with many of them through their struggles I've become slightly less repulsed. I may even be manifesting signs of compassion toward their "plight." Things are not always as they appear. What looks like sheer laziness may not be. In many cases, these sloth-like creatures secretly struggle with self-confidence. It's not lethargy that holds them back. It's fear. They're afraid of failure. They're afraid of responsibility. The prospect of pain involved in making choices is too much for them to overcome. Yet to advance you have to make decisions. Many men, unwilling to get up and face their responsibility, decide not to decide.

To put that another way, many young men (and old) choose not to succeed by choosing to do nothing. They take the path of least resistance. Many men are in a line of work simply because it required nothing of them. Such is the reason so many men find themselves in unfulfilling careers somewhere down the road. They were unwilling to match their natural ambitions with the discipline it takes to achieve them.

Fundamentally, they were more afraid of failing than they were committed to succeeding. Later in life, they regret not having tried. As kids they faced the classic question—"What do you want to be when you grow up?"—with hope and promise. Forty years later they're still trying to answer it. They still don't know who they are.

This is the very reason so many wives grow frustrated by their husbands just a few short years into marriage. Thinking they were marrying a man, they soon realize he's a boy emotionally. Wives kick against his lethargy. This is because they are conditioned by God to depend on their husbands' motivation for life. In the absence of this quality, wives end up picking up the slack or becoming their husbands' life coaches. Eventually, wives lose respect. Eventually, husbands lose the reins.

THE RAREST OF SPECIES

The rarest and most enviable creature of all is the man who loves what he does. The guy who has found the certain thing he is "supposed" to do. It's a self-evident quality. There's a consistency about him that comes from doing what he's supposed to do. Confidence. I don't mean an enthusiasm for the mundane realities within industries and careers— products, money, strategic planning—but what underlies these things: integrity, vision, aptitude, progress, relationships. They are driven by the thrill of leadership, accomplishing a task, overcoming obstacles, the details involved in quality and the awareness that they are contributing to something larger than themselves.

Ambition is not a bad thing. It's not always arrogant and prideful as many people assume. For sure, it can be. There are ugly versions of it. But there is also a type of ambition that is healthy and humble. It results from a unique combination of ingredients: personal clarity, self-assuredness, restraint, passion, and conviction. Young men need this type of ambition to be productive members of society. They need to cultivate godly ambition to find their way.

Ambition is not the same as having a dream. A dream is simply the raw material for aim and purpose. The dreamer is the guy who would like to do something without a clue as to how to do it. A dream is good to have, but usually isn't tempered by reality. Dreamers frustrate those around them by false starts and wasted resources. A wise decision is what happens when a dream has looked reality in the face. It's an awareness of what one can do in light of the cost involved in doing it. True ambition has both the courage and wisdom to get the dream off the ground.

"You can do anything you set your mind to" may be the most frequent bad advice parents give their children. It's untrue and misleading. I know parents are simply trying to encourage their kids, but you can't actually do anything you set your mind to. (Come play golf with me. I'll prove it.) God gives people different gifts and capacities. Some people are simply better at some things than others. In every single case a person's makeup limits his ability to succeed in certain things. Fact is, we're not good at everything. We can't actually do everything we set our minds to. What we should be telling our kids is, "You can try to do nearly anything. But you can succeed only in what you should be doing."

Case in point. I know a young man who dreamed of joining the Marine Corps. An athletic, self-disciplined, well-rounded kid totally committed to his goal. He never wavered from this career path throughout his adolescence. Just prior to his high school graduation he walked into the recruitment office to enlist. With a lifelong goal within reach, he was rejected because of a failed hearing exam. Some things you can't control. Which is the point.

LET'S GO FIND IT TOGETHER

Every parent wants his or her child to succeed. But our job is not to encourage them to pursue anything they want. Our job is to guide them in the discovery of what they should pursue. Part of being a dad is helping your son discover his calling in life. We're sounding boards and sources of encouragement as they explore various interests and paths. We have the best view of their life. The Marine Corps is not the most important thing, but the features of this young man's life drove him toward it—duty, discipline, etc. These qualities can be applied to a multiplicity of pursuits that have nothing to do with a career in the military. They are not contingent upon hearing exams. If a dad has done his job, his son will already know this.

Dads can struggle at this particular point. In an attempt to push their sons, they end up frustrating them rather than liberating them. Many try to live vicariously through their sons, thrusting their personal ambition on them. This usually results in aggravation for the son. Other dads push them down some path they prefer with brute force. This never works. But it is possible to help our sons make prudent decisions without discouraging their zeal. It's a matter of directing their ambition and not trying to control outcomes. We have to help them understand who they are before they can understand what they should do.

Our aim should be to help our sons locate their capacity, not decide how or where they should apply it. We don't decide what they are to do, but we do help them understand what they should be doing. We have to pay close attention to the nuance of their personalities if we're going to do this. We have to be engaged if we're going to help them discover their calling.

I have a friend who is a rheumatologist. (If you did not pay attention in biology, he helps old people with their joints.) What's more, he specializes in treating gout. Because he's a close friend, I know more about gout than I ever wanted to know. The guy is obsessed. Every conversation at nearly every occasion inevitably heads toward this unpleasant-sounding ailment. Despite the fact that gout makes for terrible dinner conversation, his passion is illustrative. I'm rather certain he never dreamed of becoming a rheumatologist specializing in the treatment of gout when he was eight. (If he did, that too is a whole 'notha chapter.) But regardless of the path that led him to this field, what's most important is why he does it. It's not the buildup of uric acid that grips him. He finds the greatest satisfaction in helping relieve the excruciating pain brought on by a much-misunderstood ailment. He found his niche. He *is* a gout doctor.

I've seen dads pull their hair out over a son's lack of motivation. It's a frequent point of contention and the source of many strained father-son relationships. Like the ubiquitous dad who struggles with his son's lack of interest in sports. I see this nut every weekend at my own sons' sporting events. However this pressure is manifested, sons end up rejecting their dad's counsel, feeling as if they'll never live up to his standards. Dads end up saying things like, "I don't care what you do, just do something!" What they should have said a long time ago is, "I care about what you want to do. Now let's go find out what that is."

My father struggled with my calling to ministry. He was concerned about everything a father would normally be concerned about. Ministry is hard. Despite his reservations, he encouraged me along the way. Some time later, well into my ministry, he took me aside and said, "I get it. Watching what you do makes total sense. This is what you're supposed to be doing." Every son wants to hear his father say this. There's a world of freedom in these words.

It's far more exhilarating to watch a son work hard at something he believes in rather than see him trudge unhappily through what we preferred. Which brings me to the point: Many young men choose not to succeed simply because they've not discovered what they should be doing. A dad's job is to set his son up for success by helping him discover what this is. When the kid finds it, the rest takes care of itself.

R.E. LEE'S LETTER TO HIS SON

Arlington House, April 5, 1852

My dear son:

I am just in the act of leaving for New Mexico. My fine old regiment has been ordered to that distant region, and I must hasten to see that they are properly taken care of. I have but little to add in reply to your letter of March 26. Your letters breathe a true spirit of frankness; they have given myself and your mother great pleasure.

You must study to be frank with the world; frankness is the child of honest courage. Say what you mean to do on every occasion, and take it for granted you mean to do right. If a friend should ask a favor, you should grant it, if it is possible and reasonable, if not, tell him plainly why you cannot. You will wrong him and yourself by equivocation of any kind. Never do a wrong thing to make a friend or keep one. The man who requires you to do so is dearly purchased at a sacrifice.

Deal kindly but firmly with all your classmates. You will find it the policy which wears best. Above all do not appear to others what you are not. If you have any fault to find with anyone, tell him, not others, of what you complain. There is no more dangerous experiment than that of undertaking to be one thing before a man's face and another behind his back. We should live and act and say nothing to injure of anyone. It is not only best as a matter of principle but it is the path to peace and honor.

In regard to duty, let me in conclusion of this hasty letter, inform you that nearly a hundred years ago there was a day of remarkable gloom and darkness, still known as the dark day, a day when the light of the sun was slowly extinguished as if by an eclipse. The legislature of Connecticut was in session and as its members saw the unexpected and unaccountable darkness coming on, they shared in the general awe and terror. It was supposed by many that the day of judgment had come.

Someone in the consternation of the hour moved for an adjournment. Then there arose an old patriotic legislator, Davenport of

Stamford, who said that if the last day had come, he desired to be found in his place of duty, and therefore moved that candles be brought in so that the house could proceed with its duty. There was quietness in that man's mind, the quietness of heavenly wisdom, an inflexible willingness to obey his duty. Duty, then is the sublimest word in our language. Do your duty in all things, like the old puritan. You cannot do more, you should never wish to do less. Let not me or your mother wear one gray hair for any lack of duty on your part.

Your affectionate father,
R. E. LEE.
to G. W. Custis Lee.

6

SINCERITY: IT'S THE *WHY* THAT MATTERS MOST

Who may ascend into the hill of the LORD? And who may stand in His holy place? He who has clean hands and a pure heart, who has not lifted up his soul to falsehood, and has not sworn deceitfully. He shall receive a blessing from the LORD and righteousness from the God of his salvation.

{ PSALM 24:3-5 }

The most expensive painting to ever sell sold for $140 million. It was a work by Jackson Pollock. The most valuable paintings in my house are works done in crayon and pencil. I have hundreds of them. I often find them on my pillow at night. Even though the depictions of me usually have a disproportionately large head, I love them. It's a good moment when I walk into my bedroom at night to find one of them waiting for me. Obviously they're valuable to me because of who painted them. But more importantly they're valuable because of why they were painted. It's the "why" that makes them priceless to me.

The same principle applies to the Christian life. You can't simply go through the motions as a Christian and assume you're done. You have to mean it. You have to want to do it. Sincerity is the true test of what we place before God. It's easy to convince ourselves we're doing well enough. That is, until someone or something stops us and reminds us to ask deeper questions of ourselves. "Why are we doing what we're doing?" That question changes everything.

From the outset let me make this clear: You can't actually fulfill the great commandment. You won't and you never have. Since Adam took the legs out from under humanity in the fall, no one has been able to love God with all his heart, mind, and soul. Sin makes this impossible. Besides, despite what most people assume, the greatest commandment is not the standard of Christianity. Jesus Christ is. Jesus Christ died to save me from the consequences of failing to obey that commandment. Furthermore, Jesus fulfilled it. The gospel is my "commandment." I am righteous before God because of what someone else has done. This I confess.

Nonetheless, God, by His grace, has opened my eyes. I now see the truth. By His grace He is conforming me into the image of His glorious Son. By the Spirit's power I am able to obey, although imperfectly, with a heart that desires to please Him. "The wanting is there," as Paul said (see Romans 7:18). I am now face-to-face with the insincerity of my fallen heart before Him. I know that only grace sustains me. Out of love for my Savior and my God I am compelled to do what I do from a pure heart. This principle undergirds my every obedience. I do not work to accomplish what has been accomplished for me. I have new reason to obey. In this I am constantly circling back to this question: Why?

LESS IS MORE

This reality is easy enough to prove. Take, for instance, a wife who has numerous responsibilities in marriage. The question isn't "Is she submitting to her husband?" The real question is "Does she *want* to submit to her husband?" She has to want to. Does she desire to honor God and her husband by willingly submitting to God's role for her life? Husbands can tell the difference.

Consider a husband. The question isn't "Is he a leader?" but "Does he take pleasure in sacrificing his own needs to meet those of his wife?" There are plenty of men who fail to lead their wives. But there are also men who think they are leaders whose efforts never really rise above the level of a supervisor. The difference is sincerity. Wives can tell the difference.

Think about young adults and purity. The question is not "Are you chaste?" Impurity is a matter of the heart. The real question is "Why are you chaste?" Because of moral pressure? Because your parents and peers keep a close eye on you? Or because you believe what God has said about sex? The fulfillment that comes from obeying God's design for the physical relationship is the greatest joy.

What about service? The question is not "Are you serving?" but "Why are you serving?" Yeah…everyone should. Everyone has a role to play. But service has to go beyond this if it is to be true. Otherwise our motivations end in guilt or the need for approval. The real question is "Are you willing to serve the greater good of Christ and others even to the point of sacrificing personal recognition because it brings our Lord glory?"

It's always a matter of motive. Whether wife, husband, or servant, the only motive that stands the test of time and trials is wholehearted sincerity to God. Otherwise, a wife will grow bitter when her husband does not reciprocate. A husband will be negligent when he is not respected. A young person will become promiscuous when all he or she is doing is surviving until marriage. Our service will be conditional and begrudging if we are not appreciated.

All of this is altered and made right when we want to do it. You can always tell when a person does what he's supposed to do simply because he has a heart that wants to please his heavenly Father. It changes the quality of a thing. It draws people to it. Sincerity turns bitterness to joy, resentment to compassion, and frustration to hope. "When a man's ways are pleasing to the LORD, He makes even his enemies to be at peace with him" (Proverbs 16:7).

That expression "heart, soul, and mind" that we're so familiar with is an idiom. It's a way of saying love God with everything you have. Heart *our* affections. Soul *our* will. Mind *our* intentions. That is a wholehearted love for God. That is a powerful thing. So powerful Jesus tells us the whole Law is fulfilled by it: "On these two commandments depend the whole Law and the Prophets" (Matthew 22:40). This, of course, is what He did on the cross.

That's a remarkable statement. It would have been a mind-blowing principle to His audience. They assumed you get to the point of pleasing God by doing what you are required to do. Love the Lord your God with all your heart reverses that. You do what you are required to do when you have taken pleasure in God.

It's a simplicity that accomplishes what we can't by trying harder. When our hearts are pure, everything we normally worry about getting right gets done. It's the difference between studying the Bible to learn about God and studying the Bible because you are satisfied in God. It's why a repentant tax collector standing next to an accomplished Pharisee in the temple turns out to be the only true worshiper around.

REVERSING WHAT WE GET BACKWARD

This love for God reverses what we get backward. Take lust. Rather than merely struggling against our desires for the wrong thing, we desire something more desirable. Rather than pleading with God to help us love our spouses as we should, our love for God results in our being the kind of spouses who please God and encourage our mates. This is why Jesus said, "The second is like it, 'You shall love your neighbor as yourself'" (Matthew 22:39). A wholehearted love for God changes how we live. The greatest measure of our sincere love toward God is our love for others.

When you sin against your spouse, the real problem is not your love for your spouse, but your love for God. I have never seen a marriage saved from the brink of divorce because someone decided to love his spouse more, but because someone realized he did not love God enough. Because he fell short of sincere love for God and found it in repentance.

The nation of Israel—following a forty-year trek around the desert—stood on the edge of promise. There were hundreds of duties awaiting them on the other side. But the totality of their obligation and survival came down to one thing: whether they meant it or not. Was their service from a heart of love for God? You can hear Moses warn of the danger of insincerity in his words to the people: "…watch yourself, that you do not forget the LORD who brought you from the land of Egypt, out of the house of slavery. You shall fear only the LORD your God; and you shall worship Him and swear by His name" (Deuteronomy 6:12-13).

Israel was about to encounter pagan religion on a scale they could not imagine. Canaan was littered with false gods. There were gods for everything from sex to agriculture. A feature central to each god was its total disregard for the motive of its worshiper. *Idols do not care why you place a sacrifice at their feet.* They care only that you do so in the prescribed way, at the prescribed time, for the prescribed effect. Ultimately it was the superficiality of paganism that posed the greatest threat to the nation's existence. Should they ever approach the living God this way, the outcome would be tragic.

But the Lord God is one. He is not one among many. The Lord created and is over all things. He has no need of anything. There is nothing we can give Him that He did not create. The only thing we have to give Him, which is already His, is the entirety of our lives, our hearts. Unlike those dead idols, Yahweh is a living God who can look right into the hearts of His people. No matter what He might require us to do, what will always matter most is why we do it. Motive has always been everything. It will always be everything.

A LIBERATING SIMPLICITY

Hundreds of years later, when asked to pinpoint the greatest commandment, Jesus quoted Moses' message. By this time, the Law had been complicated and codified into an unrecognizable mass of rules and regulations. People were responsible to keep track of a to-do list with some 700 items on it. The question was supposedly too complicated to satisfy. It was the needle in a haystack of religion: "When the Pharisees heard that Jesus had silenced the Sadducees, they gathered themselves together. One of them, a lawyer, asked Him a question, testing Him, 'Teacher, which is the great commandment in the Law?'" (Matthew 22:34-36).

Because the Pharisees expected Jesus would need some time to figure this out, they must have been shocked when the answer came right back. His reply cut through all the sophisticated religious rhetoric. He found the needle. Without hesitation He answered, "Love God." He said, "You shall love the Lord your God with all your heart, and with all your soul, and with all your mind. This is the great and foremost commandment" (verse 37).

What's impressive is the absence of any complexity. What makes Jesus' declaration so powerful is not a complexity, but a simplicity even a child could grasp. Love God. That type of simplicity is liberating. It puts everything in the right order. Ultimately it is the only way to live.

As I've parented my children, I've tried to approach them in the same way. My target has not been their performance, or compliance, but their hearts. I'm not aiming at superficial realities. I'm aiming at deeper ones. I want them to learn their own hearts and the struggles that lie within. I don't want them arguing with me, but with their own consciences before God. I won't always be there to apply external pressure. I have to hand them a motive that goes beyond consequences. The pros far outnumber the cons here.

Heartfelt sincerity relieves us of the burden of performance. I don't have to remember a hundred little rules. Rather, I have to remember only one reality, Christ, and one opportunity, love God. "I will praise the name of God with song, and magnify Him with thanksgiving. And it will please the LORD better than an ox or a young bull with horns and hoofs" (Psalm 69:30-31).

Sincerity gives all our efforts at personal change a greater meaning. It's one thing to need discipline. It's another thing altogether to realize that pursuing personal discipline is pleasing to God because in the end it allows us to dedicate more of ourselves to Him. "Before I was afflicted I went astray, but now I keep Your word" (Psalm 119:67).

Love for God simplifies our most complicated issues. We always know where to look when things are amiss in our lives. When David found himself drowning in troubles, he knew the source of them all: "Against You, You only, I have sinned" (Psalm 51:4). We always know where to repent first.

Sincerity removes guilt as a motive for my service to God. I no longer do what I do because I have to, but because I want to. I have nothing I need to accomplish. Christ has done that for me. I am free to obey.

It ensures that all we do is an offering to God and not an attempt at appeasing Him. What we do now becomes one constant offering to God. "Now if any man builds on the foundation with gold, silver, precious stones, wood, hay, straw, each man's work will become evident; for the day will show it because it is to be revealed with fire, and the fire itself will test the quality of each man's work" (1 Corinthians 3:12-13).

A focus on the heart promotes a healthy self-awareness that guides us through life and all of its many issues. It causes us to ask ourselves deeper questions about our motives and intentions.

7

ACCOUNTABILITY: YOU ARE NOT
YOUR OWN BEST COUNSELOR

There is a friend who sticks closer than a brother.
{ PROVERBS 18:24 }

Men are notoriously bad at friendships. Wait, that's too gener-
ous. Actually, we're pathetic at being a friend. Either we sur-
round ourselves with a group of "men" or "guys" who help keep the
bar safely within reach (this way we can feel good about ourselves), or
we isolate ourselves (this way we don't have to deal with it). In the first
instance, we're never challenged as we dwell safely in mediocrity. In the
second instance, no one ever gets in to see the truth. If someone did get
in, the exposure would be too embarrassing. In either case, it's a recipe
for immaturity and stagnation.

Not buddies, mind you, but friends. There's a difference. Buddies
are the guys who come over to your house in your first year of marriage to play Madden while your wife seeks refuge in the bedroom
behind laundry and bills. Buddies are the guys who resent their marriage and want you to resent yours as well. Buddies are the morons who
provide you the excuse needed to avoid your responsibilities—invit-
ing you to the fantasy draft or the poker night or the boccie ball tour-
nament. Buddies sit around and tolerate your narcissism. Buddies are
the guys who call to inform you that Apple will soon release the third-
generation iPad. "We're gonna camp out!" (Relax—there's no new iPad
being released.) You had buddies when you were eight. You're not eight.

It's wrong to operate with friends on surface levels. It's disingenuous and dishonest to pass the time in friendships serving up platitudes and niceties. But this is usually where we live. Think of all the people you call friends. How well do you know them? Where's their hometown? Where did they meet their wives? What are their deep-heart struggles? How often do you pray for them? We don't really know each other. We treat the souls around us so haphazardly.

> Let us hold fast the confession of our hope without waver-
> ing, for He who promised is faithful; and let us consider
> how to stimulate one another to love and good deeds, not
> forsaking our own assembling together, as is the habit of
> some, but encouraging one another; and all the more as
> you see the day drawing near (Hebrews 10:23-25).

I realize time is limited and we are busy. I get that. There are greater and more pressing priorities to which we must attend: God, family, children, work, etc. Despite this, if you are too busy for friendships, you are too busy. You need to loosen up your schedule and your life. You're cutting yourself off from the immeasurable blessing of the Christian life.

HOW'S WHAT'S-HIS-NAME?

I was sitting around with two friends fellowshipping over pizza not too long ago. Collectively, we'd known each other about eight years at the time. As we talked, one friend asked about the other friend's son. He got his name wrong in the process. "My son's name is John," the dad retorted. It was awkward. Crickets…I fell out laughing. Like any true friend would. So as to memorialize this glorious blunder, I get his name wrong every time I see them. But this slipup illustrates the point. We don't really pay attention to each other's lives.

If we were forced to delete one little word from our vocabulary, we'd be much better at the art of friendship. The word? *Fine.* We hide behind this word, and its many synonyms, like an impenetrable defense against being known. Anymore, it's the extent of our conversations. "How are things?" "Oh, they're fine." It is way overused. So much so, it usually signals the exact opposite of what we intend to communicate. Things aren't fine.

Imagine the exposure if you were not allowed to use it for an entire week. "How are you?" "Actually, I've been struggling with anger." "My wife and I are not doing well at present." "To be honest, my spiritual life has stalled out." Or, on a more positive note, "God has been giving great victory over anger lately." "My spiritual life has been so rich. How's yours?" "I've been repenting of poor leadership in my relationship with my wife." This is the stuff friendships are made of. Friendships are real.

I have several acquaintances who live in the touch-and-go world of big business. Occasionally they schedule lunch with me. After all, I'm the pastor of the church they "attend." In their line of work they're used to having "the man's" ear. I usually oblige. As I sit with them, I can't help but feel like a potential sale or an employee. The plastic is suffocating. It's amazing what living from one handshake to the next over decades can do to a man. Everyone they "befriend" feels as if they were inserted into some pipeline of a potential sale.

At lunch the agenda is queued up. Usually it's prepared by the wife. All the transitions are timed. We solve his marital problems and child's behavior issues in under thirty minutes. They fight me for the check. We're "eighty-eight and out the gate" in under an hour. They have no idea how bad it is. I pray for them when I get in my car. They mark me off their agenda in theirs. It's such an opaque existence.

FRIENDS DON'T LET FRIENDS GET AWAY WITH STUPIDITY

Point is, true friendships are sincere, not scheduled. Friendship bears certain characteristics. Hard stops are not one of them.

Transparency. Friendship demands honesty and recognizes attempts to obscure. Not that it has to know everything, or even expects to, but it allows for it. A friend knows who you truly are and is a friend anyway.

Grace. It gives the benefit of the doubt even when it's hard. It's not conditional. It does not abandon the scene when a failure occurs. On the contrary, it's the first to show.

Truth. It does not let your weaknesses off the hook. It does not make excuses for your excuses. It survives confrontation. If it sees something it goes after it, but it always has your best interest in mind. It confronts with a healthy offering of the benefit of the doubt. It leaves a friendship better than it found it.

Love. It asks deeper questions than you're comfortable with. The question which goes deeper than "How are you?" It gets nervous when you fall beneath the radar. It serves you beyond your expectations. Sometimes beyond your comfort level.

Change. Its aim is to encourage conformity to your Lord. It is inherent in church. Oftentimes you can trace spiritual immaturity back to men who have not been investing themselves in friendships at the local church level.

Over the years, God has blessed me with some amazing friendships. They span decades. In every case, these friendships have manifested all the above features at one time or another. I have confronted and been confronted. I have pursued and been pursued. I have loved and been loved—despite failure. I have mocked and been mocked for stupid insecurities. I have prayed and been prayed over. I have confessed and listened. I have forgiven and been forgiven. I have served and been served.

THE INDELIBLE MARKS OF LOVE

There have been some incredible men who have stepped up in my world over the years, risking friendship and respect to help me. I remember distinctly as a teenager my Uncle Mike asking me to come over and help him "trim some shrubs" in his front yard. It was a total setup. He lovingly confronted some rebellion that had begun to manifest itself in my life. It turned my heart.

I was in seminary in Los Angeles, California during the 1994 earthquake. I panicked. I came face-to-face with the weakness of my faith. I withdrew from school and was headed home. Most of my "friends" gave me passes. "We understand. God can use you anywhere. Good luck." Except one friend—Patrick. His approach was a little more direct. "Don't be a pansy. This is the gospel we're serving here. Suck it up! You've not suffered to the point of shedding blood!" I would not be writing this today if it weren't for his love.

Then there's Jackie, who stepped in when my dad died and filled a gap few others could. With unbelievable perception he saw the need and filled it. We speak twice a week. He is the man with whom I've shared my darkest moments without fear. And there's Bob—thirty years my senior—who took me under his wings and taught me how to be a leader. And Guy, who taught me what true service looks like. Doug and his attention to detail. Christian and his fearless confrontation of all my "great ideas." Danny and a level of compassion I could only hope to have. The list goes on and on.

I have taken something from each man along the way. In one way or another these friendships have shaped me. From one, a sensitivity that I needed to develop in my own life. From another, an approach to decision making that was filled with wide-eyed realism and hope. Their marks are all over my life.

Most men rarely have one friend like these, much less five. One is invaluable. More than one is a treasure. You can count your real friends on one hand.

Excuses abound as to why no friendships exist. None are valid. "I don't have time" could equally mean we're too selfish. We have life pursuits that don't easily accommodate other people. "I don't have anything to contribute" really means we're too insecure. Since we don't normally expose our true hearts to other people, we fear rejection. "There's no one with whom I have anything in common" really means we cannot overcome the awkwardness of putting ourselves out there. But the rewards of overcoming every excuse far exceed the losses. Friendships are a source of grace that can only come from attaching yourself to men who are struggling through the same challenges as you. This bond is invaluable.

For one, these friendships are a constant *sanity check*. Without them, you can get isolated real fast, especially in the midst of a trial. You can go crazy out there by yourself. Friends walk with you when a crisis unexpectedly stops by your world. They let you know you're not crazy.

They're also a *gut check*. We have the potential for making some really bad decisions. We can convince ourselves that the most asinine logic is foolproof genius. Without these people checking us, we can put our family and futures at risk. Friends loan you their "sanity buzzer" when yours is broken.

These friendships are also a *reality check*. They provide us objectivity when examining self. Our judgment is usually clouded when it comes to rightly assessing our own sin. Our counsel most always leans in our favor and lets us off the hook. We are not our own best counselors. The true friend helps us see about us what we can't see by ourselves.

Someone once wrote that our best friends are those who make us most afraid to sin. There's a lot of truth to this statement. I take it to mean that our best friends are those who help us face who we truly are and force us to deal with it. The standard of their life and conduct make us want to elevate ours. In this way, our best friends are the severest enemies of our complacency.

GETTING FRIENDS ON THE AGENDA

Men hide themselves from the exposure of friendship by stepping behind various—and very predictable—façades. These are the versions of themselves they want people to believe are real. They are the devices that keep people at arm's length. There is the comic. Everything is a joke and every joke is a deflection. There is the misfit. The guy who never grew up and hides behind his delinquency. There is the businessman. He's too busy for anyone else. He's getting it done while the rest of us are sucking wind. There is the quiet man. He just doesn't like to open up. There's the man's man. Being transparent with other men is a sign of weakness. There's the plastic man. Apparently he doesn't have any problems. As the saying goes, if you're going to hide, make sure it's behind something bigger than your issues. Hey, dude! We can see you.

Right now you are probably convicted. You're saying to yourself, "I need some friends. I'm going to get some. I'll add it to my agenda. What steps should I take? Where's the book on this?" Okay dude, here's the deal. If you have to read a book or need twelve steps on how to make friends, you have far more serious problems. Friendship is about the most natural thing we're capable of as human beings.

Others of you are thinking you've been a good friend and have true friendships. You have a group of guys you meet with every week. They know about your life. You talk openly. But have you been a friend at all? Have you actually been honest with one another, or just endured one another? Have you seen things in your brother's life and let them go? Are there blind spots he's unaware of because you've never pointed them out? After years of conversations, have you merely beat around the bushes of each other's soul, or dug them up? Why haven't you said anything? "I don't want to be hurtful." But that is not a picture of biblical love. Biblical love is both intrusive and delicate. "It's none of my business." Obviously we're not the Holy Spirit and many issues are not our business, but we are called to be instruments of change in the lives of others. The fear of man keeps our love and concern at an unhealthy distance. Men suffer blind spots for decades because "friends" are "too nice" to point them out. After all, things are "fine."

> Speaking the truth in love, we are to grow up in all aspects into Him who is the head, even Christ, from whom the whole body, being fitted and held together by that which every joint supplies, according to the proper working of each individual part, causes the growth of the body for the building up of itself in love (Ephesians 4:15-16).

There could be other reasons men don't invest in friendships. Maybe they have something to hide. Namely, themselves. Some men may be too embarrassed to expose the realities lurking in their personal and spiritual life. The shallowness of their soul. The ineptitude with the basics of the Christian life. They don't know how to lead their wives. Their finances are a mess. They are a failure in business. Etc. Uncovering their struggles to another person seems the most frightening prospect they can imagine. Squaring with reality would be the hardest thing they've ever done. The risk is too great.

Wives—who are experts at friendship—hurt for their husbands when the bonds of Christian friendships are missing. It's not uncommon for the wives to reach out to me, as their pastor, in an effort to help. Like covert operatives—not wanting to embarrass their husbands—they approach me and share their husband's struggle with me. "Please don't tell him we talked; he'd be so upset." They have no clue how they are enabling their husband's condition by approaching the problem this way. "Lonely," "isolated," and "depressed" are some of the ways they describe their man.

Usually the solution they have in mind is for me to become their husband's "B.F.F." "How about asking him to lunch?" Honestly, the logic is a little off for me. Their husband struggles to make friends and reach out to others. For him, the thought of doing so fills him with anxiety. Therefore, the wife determines the logical thing to do is arrange a lunch with the one man her husband fears most—his pastor. It begins with an awkward handshake at the door, a few "I'm fines," and an average salad. What results is typical.

My strategy is to be normal. An average guy—which I am—and not the "holy man on campus" they think I am. Same struggles, pains, shortcomings as any man. A man dependent on the same grace as any other man. Normal is the best thing I can do for them. It usually takes them by surprise. They expect Thees and Thous to be coming out of my mouth. What they get are batting averages and tools down at Lowes. Usually they are blown away by how normal it all was. More lunches result. He shares more of what's really going on his life. Connections are made. A friendship is born.

It's a joy to encourage men. What happens in these moments is a unique type of encouragement. When these men discover their pastor is an ordinary guy whom God's grace redeemed and put into service, they begin to make the connection of God's grace to their own lives. Literally, if God can use Byron, He can use me.

Point is, establishing friendships is not complicated. But it is hard on a man's ego. In order to have friendships there are some painful things you have to do.

Die to self. Friendships require humility. You have to put down your pride—which is usually at the core—and put yourself out there with others. Some of the most prideful men I know are also some of the most quiet. The result is distance and isolation. They're so wrapped up in the perception of others and fear of men they choose to hide in their insecurities. Fundamentally, this is a failure to believe the truth of the gospel. Who cares about your deficiencies and social awkwardness? What difference does all that make anyway in God's economy? God's grace is sufficient for these things.

Serve. Friendships are born out of an attitude of self-sacrifice and service. Most people approach friendship selfishly. We seek out friends because of what they can provide us, or because we have things in common. They fit our interests. When they don't provide what we want or fail to meet our expectations, the friendship suffers. That's not real friendship. Real friendship is not about us. It's born out of a heart of service to others. Pardon me for being so direct, but not having friends is selfish. There are other people to consider. People—otherwise known as friends—who could benefit from your gifts and service. Choosing to rest in the margin is being self-absorbed.

Most of my closest friends are the result of our service one to another. At some point in our lives, someone tied on the apron of a servant and took a basin and served another person in the throes of their need. Bonds of compassionate trust were formed in these moments that transcend all those things which usually keep us at arm's length.

If you so choose, you can run from friendships and the accountability they bring. You can hesitate before the awkwardness. But you need friends. What's more, there are others who need you. And you know it. No matter how far and fast you can run, you will never outrun the need for other people.

8

CONFIDENCE: BE COMFORTABLE IN YOUR OWN SKIN

Whom have I in heaven but You? And besides You, I desire nothing on earth. My flesh and my heart may fail, but God is the strength of my heart and my portion forever. For, behold, those who are far from You will perish; You have destroyed all those who are unfaithful to You. But as for me, the nearness of God is my good; I have made the Lord GOD my refuge, that I may tell of all Your works.

{ PSALM 73:25-28 }

S o much is made right when a man is comfortable in his own skin. It's a very discernible quality. A sort of ease. A resting. A placid disposition not needing to rise above or fall below where it is. You know it when you see it. I remember, even as a young child, sensing it in my grandfather, Brock Crain Sr. My visual is a tall, handsome man who smelled of St. John's Bay Rum Cologne and reclined in a red-leather easy chair with a six-pipe tobacco station at the ready. I never wondered who he was. Obviously I knew he was my grandfather, but I never doubted the *kind* of man he was. He was among the most consistent things I knew. I always had a sense of safety when I was near him. I'm sure we all feel the same way about our grandfathers. I suppose by the time a man reaches his eighties he's given up trying to be something he's not.

In a good sense, these men are always the same man. Not stagnant, mind you, but steady. Not monotonous, or boring, but predictable. There's no mystery about them. They have a humble "what you see is what you get" air. To know them is to know the man. It's not arrogance, but transparency. They've beheld themselves and are comfortable with what they see. They admire and learn from the capacities of others, but don't feel inferior to them. They've come to terms with who they are. There is a freedom in such a man.

The hallmark is confidence—a quality I'm certain we misunderstand. Confidence isn't blind self-assuredness. It's wide-eyed humility. Confidence is knowing you're not good at everything, and being okay with it. A confident man admits he lacks proficiency in certain things and doesn't pretend he has it. He is comfortable with his limitations. If he's sitting around with friends—all of whom dabble in quantum physics—he doesn't act as if he knows what string theory is. "Ah yes, string theory. It's my favorite type of musical composition." He sits there quietly and learns, or waits for the topic to turn. Or thinks of string cheese instead.

These guys aren't rattled by what others think of them. I don't mean to suggest they're indifferent to the opinions of others. What I mean is the opinions of others neither bristle nor corrupt them. Criticisms—even those intended to wound—are viewed as useful for the building of character. If change will make him better, he's not afraid to face it. After all, he's seen his sin up close. He benefits from people observing about him what he already knows to be true. It's a "checking of his six o'clock." His critics are miffed when he agrees with them. "So, you've noticed that? Pesky imperfection. Thanks for pointing it out."

Compliments—even those offered sincerely—don't go to his head. For the same reasons criticisms don't get to his pride, *his sin*. He is well aware that any good in his life is from God. Compliments could go to his head only if he were dishonest about who he was. They would corrupt him only if this life were some illusion. We've all seen the person who waves off a compliment in false piety. (Note: Read the following with King James inflection.) "Thank you, but I cannot accept that. It is the Most Holy God who deserves to be honored. Not me." Inside he's begging for more. The guy we're talking about—the one who's sure of himself—receives the same compliment, says "Thanks," and doesn't take it too seriously. Both compliments and condemnations humble him.

Most men are controlled by what others think of them. A fear of man dominates them. Rather than resting comfortably in who they are, they project versions of themselves they want others to believe in. They spend their lives reinforcing the deception. In one way or another, these men are always angling toward a preferred likeness. It comes out in all kinds of ways. A refusal to admit wrong. An unwillingness to ask for help. An obnoxious desire for affirmation. An overstatement of accomplishments. A desire to get the last word in. An inability to play well with others. A poorly timed joke that shuts down a room. A sarcasm that has a faint vindictiveness about it. A wit that keeps people at a safe distance.

A VERSION OF THE MAN THEY WISH THEY WERE

Over time these men forget what's perception and what's reality. They become versions of themselves. They become "one-up artists." There's one in every crowd. Every time others share a life experience, he steps on their last word in an effort to outshine them. As if everyone else's life is an opening act for his. "Thanks Bob, I'll take it from here. That's nothing really. I once had to perform a tracheotomy on a squirrel. I used my gold-nibbed Montblanc." Or it's the now-infamous softball guy. That fella who takes himself too seriously and wears spikes to church-league softball. He's convinced the only reason he's not in the majors is early career decisions. He's a hundred other versions of the same guy everyone else hurts for.

You can see where the insecurity comes from. As others begin to realize the distance between perception and reality they grow defensive. Like when a wife has to weigh every word (and butter the ones she uses) in order to inquire about some basic responsibility. "Sweetheart, otherwise known as the most amazing man I've ever met, did you pay the gas bill? I'm just asking because it's cold in here and the heat is not working. I'm happy to build a fire in the den as an alternative. I only wanted to know." He's so afraid she'll see his incompetence he barks at her in anger, "Why do you have to criticize me like that?" Fact is he did forget to pay the bill. He has forgotten frequently. Rather than admit that he's irresponsible and do something about it, he retreats into the refuge of his denial.

This is exhausting. It takes a lot of time and energy to be this bogus. After a while it's utterly frustrating. Way down the road of their lives these men grow resentful or give up. At other times they lurch back and forth between various aspirations, hoping one of them will do the trick. *Discontent* may be the best word to use to describe them. They're engulfed in a sort of lostness. They think they're looking for some*thing* when in actuality they're hiding from some*one*—themselves. Most of them don't even see it. It's obvious to everyone else. It makes you hurt for them.

Why is it necessary for us to project these things? Why aren't we content with who we are? Why must we force this struggle on those around us? Why do we make people walk on eggshells? What is it we want others to believe about us? Why all this nonsense? It's madness.

THE COMB-OVER

Insecurity is the anxiety resulting from having to hide from other people what we know is true of ourselves. It's what happens when we're uncomfortable in our own skin. We shift around in ourselves like an eight-year-old in a sports coat and clip-on tie. It's awkward and it makes everyone else awkward. Insecurity, because it's often self-deprecating, can resemble meekness, but it's not. It's not a lack of confidence. It's a want of attention. Ultimately, it's selfish and prideful. It forces others to play by your rules and tiptoe around your sensibilities. No true relationships can spring up. No honest conversations can ever take place. It's always about you. It's a constant elephant in the room. It's the truth about you hiding in the wide open.

Our insecurities are like the guy with the massive comb-over. You know him. Be honest—when you see him you immediately ask, "What is he thinking? That's ridiculous! The whole world knows he's bald." The only thing the comb-over does is expose the truth about both his baldness *and* his vanity. He's going bald and he's self-conscious about it. When I see a comb-over I think *bald*. Hair is not supposed to do that.

Think about your insecurities for a moment. Those things about which you are most defensive. The bald spots in your life you cover up. (Sorry, that was metaphorical gluttony.) The many things at which you bristle. The issues your wife and friends tiptoe around. Behind those lies reality. Normally, like a comb-over, our insecurity only serves to confirm what everyone suspects. Why not just admit the reality and deal with it? "Dude, get over yourself. We all see it." We're simply too ashamed to pull back the curtain and reveal the little man behind the levers.

Okay, I'm going to take the receding hairline metaphor to the next level. I had a friend in his early fifties who had worn a hairpiece his entire life. Like all of them, it was obvious. Always there taunting us, "Hey—up here! Look at me! I'm not real!" Our conscience warns us, "For the love of friendship, don't look at it."

One day he decided he'd had enough. It came up over cards and I said, "Dude, who cares? Do what you're most comfortable with." Of course, I'm thinking to myself, *Ditch the rug, Holmes!* The following Sunday at church he walked into the sanctuary with a shiny white head leading the way. It takes a certain amount of courage to do something like that. To put it out there that way. I walked right up to him without saying a word and kissed him right on his bald head (violating every Man Law in one fell swoop). That was that.

PRECIOUS MOMENTS BETWEEN EIGHT AND TWENTY-EIGHT

A dad's job is helping his son avoid the torment of a duplicitous life. We help them create a healthy self-awareness. There are things about themselves they need to know to be effective as men—weaknesses, habits, trends, etc. Not sins necessarily, but patterns. There's no way they can see them unless someone tells them. How could they? While they're young and trusting enough to listen, we have to tell them about these things. Not in condemnatory tones, but encouraging ones. It's vitally important. A tendency to leave toys scattered in the yard when they are nine turns into financial irresponsibility when they are twenty-nine. A habit of neglecting chores when they are eleven turns into a poor work ethic at twenty-one. How can they avoid these potential shortfalls if no one ever points them out?

> My son, if you will receive my words and treasure my com-
> mandments within you, make your ear attentive to wis-
> dom, incline your heart to understanding; for if you cry
> for discernment, lift your voice for understanding; if you
> seek her as silver and search for her as for hidden treasures;
> then you will discern the fear of the LORD and discover the
> knowledge of God. For the LORD gives wisdom; from His
> mouth come knowledge and understanding. He stores up
> sound wisdom for the upright; He is a shield to those who
> walk in integrity (Proverbs 2:1-7).

The majority of men start discovering at forty what someone should
have told them at eight. By the time we realize these hidden wrinkles,
they've already done their damage. And they're hard to straighten out.
But it's liberating to finally see what others already know. To finally see
and admit the truth is healthy. It's a face-to-face with who we are. We're
sinners. Which implies imperfection. We're bent in certain areas. We
were created *with* certain abilities and *without* others. We're good at
some things and we struggle with others. That's life. Once we understand the subtleties of who we are and accept how God has made us,
we're much more at ease. Otherwise, we end up attempting to be someone we're not.

You know that no-win question on job applications that reads
something like, "What's your greatest weakness?" I hate that question. Why would I tell someone why they shouldn't hire me? No one
answers honestly anyway. We offer up self-deprecating compliments
like, "I have a hard time saying no."

Here's the deal. In order to be freed from the fear of man and be
comfortable in your own skin you have to answer it honestly for yourself. I don't mean surface answers either. I mean the "thing beneath the
thing" type of answers. I have an anger problem, goes to I'm selfish and
when people don't do exactly what I say I destroy them with words. I'm
not very patient, goes to I'm blindly arrogant and consider anyone who
makes a mistake incompetent. I don't like to open up and talk, goes to
I'm so immature and delinquent I'm embarrassed someone will see it.
I haven't found the career I want, goes to I'm too afraid to try anything

that requires strength of character. If you get it out there and deal with it, you'll know how your grandfather felt at seventy.

By the time a man reaches premarital counseling, he should know these things. There should exist an inventory. He should be able to tell his bride and counselor exactly what it is about him that will make following him a challenge. "I don't listen well. I can be self-focused and minimize others' needs. My dad showed me this when I was eight. I see it and have been dealing with it ever since." Later on when his wife notices he's looking past her to *SportsCenter* on TV as she's pouring out her heart, she can say, "You're doing that thing again" without fear of rebuttal. He can say, in return, without offering ten justifications, "Oh, sorry," and cut the tube off.

By the time a man reaches the decision of a career path, he should understand himself well enough to know which way is best. "I'm afraid of heights, so I'm not going to change light bulbs on radio towers." His sense of his abilities and inabilities guides him toward something that is suitable. This way he's protected from finding his identity in his success, or in the job itself.

By the time a man qualifies for leadership in the church, he should be balanced enough to be a team player. He does not grandstand on boards and throw himself on his sword for every issue. "Men! We are compromising the gospel. We must buy more round tablecloths." He is aware of the way in which he contributes and is secure enough to let other gifted men contribute.

DON'T BE "THAT GUY"

1. *The Left-hand Lane Guy*
    He won't move over. No matter what.

2. *Get the Last Word in Guy*
    You can't win this argument. You can't win this argument.

3. *Awkward Joke-teller Guy*
    You hurt for him. Crickets. Timing is everything.

4. *Everything's a Joke Guy*
    Hiding safely behind the punch line.

5. *Takes Himself Too Seriously Guy*
    "Battle Hymn of the Republic" plays in the background
    while he talks.

6. *"No, Please Let Me Get That" Guy*
    Inevitably, you always pick up the check.

7. *Trying to Sell Me Something Guy*
    Friendships exist for networking purposes.

8. *"Please Notice My Accomplishments" Guy*
    Every conversation is a tour through the trophy room of his life.

9. *One-up You Guy*
    You had a vasectomy. Big deal. He had two.

10. *Everything's a Competition Guy*
    Race-walking to the buffet.

11. *"Let's Get Back to Me" Guy*
    "That's good, Bob. Hope your wife recovers from brain surgery.
    Did I tell you I'm going on a cruise?"

12. *Not Ready at Airport Security Guy*
    Somehow it sneaks up on him.

13. *Name-dropper Guy*
    "Can I get that for you? I think you dropped your longing
    for significance."

14. *"Things Are Fine" Guy*
    Automatically means things are horrible.

15. *"I Don't Have Cable" Guy*
    Three local channels are next to godliness.

16. *"You'll Have to Kill Me Before I Admit I'm Wrong" Guy*
    There's no going back. "No, seriously…four plus four is nine in some countries."

17. *Pro Sports Career Delusion Guy*
    "If it weren't for my speed, hand-eye coordination, batting, fielding, and overall ability, I could have made it in the MLB."

18. *Softball Guy*
    An angry version of the Pro Sports Career Delusion Guy. Would yell at Jesus in church league softball if He missed a pop fly. Of course, that would never happen.

19. *Air Quotes Guy*
    Not everything is that dramatic.

20. *Perpetual Therapy Guy*
    The only thing missing in your relationship is the couch. Your own personal *What About Bob?*

21. *"I Have Better Stuff than You" Guy*
    "My flat-screen is 116 inches, but yours is good too."

22. *"I Can't Dress Myself" Guy*
    Biggest question each day, "Which color plaid?"

23. *Your Facts Are Slightly Off Guy*
    Letting you know he's smarter, one corrected fact at a time. You: "The space shuttle took off around noon." Him: "Actually it's the Space Transportation System Initiative Program and it took off at 12:03:39 EST."

24. *Alpha Male Guy*
    Must drive the rental car.

25. *Wears a "Smedium" Guy*
Will not go to large T-shirts. No matter what.

26. *Dead Fish Handshake Guy*
It feels sinful.

27. *Establish My Dominance Handshake Guy*
I can't feel my hand.

28. *Everything's a Debate Guy*
Yes it is. Because the opposite perspective must be represented.

29. *Thinks His Golf Game Is Better Than It Is Guy*
All worked up for nothing.

30. *Comb-over Guy*
Hey. We know.

31. *Mom's Basement Dweller Guy*
Surprisingly, no date on Friday. Again.

32. *At-the-Ready Clarifying Sports Trivia Guy*
All of a sudden, your master's degree seems useless.

33. *Adorable Misfit Guy*
Hides from responsibility behind incompetence.

34. *"I Am My Job" Guy*
Getting it done while the rest of us are sucking wind.

35. *Public Groomer Guy*
Sermons are a perfectly good time to clip one's nails.

9

MARRIAGE: IT COMES WITH A BASIN AND AN APRON

*The husband is the head of the wife, as Christ also is the head of the
church, He Himself being the Savior of the body. But as the church
is subject to Christ, so also the wives ought to be to their husbands in
everything. Husbands, love your wives, just as Christ also loved the
church and gave Himself up for her, so that He might sanctify her,
having cleansed her by the washing of water with the word, that He
might present to Himself the church in all her glory, having no spot or
wrinkle or any such thing; but that she would be holy and blameless.*

{ EPHESIANS 5:23-27 }

*Why do you look at the speck that is in your brother's eye, but do not
notice the log that is in your own eye? Or how can you say to your
brother, "Let me take the speck out of your eye," and behold, the log is
in your own eye? You hypocrite, first take the log out of your own eye,
and then you will see clearly to take the speck out of your brother's eye.*

{ MATTHEW 7:1-5 }

E veryone gets excited about a sermon series on marriage (except
single and divorced people). But everyone is excited for different reasons. It depends on which spouse we're talking about, the
husband or the wife. Husbands take pleasure in submission being reinforced. They want to see if the preacher has backbone enough to mention the dreaded *s*-word publicly. It's an ice box on the way home from
church. Wives, on the other hand, relish husbands being reminded
about the immense responsibility of spiritual leadership. They sharpen

their proverbial elbows in preparation for critical moments during the sermon. Turns out the wives have an *s*-word of their own—*servant*. It's an awkward ride on the way home.

Point is, our excitement most often has less to do with changes that might occur in us than it does with changes we want in our spouse. Our operational assumption going into a marriage series is usually the same: "My spouse really needs to hear this."

GOOD LUCK WITH THAT

Many husbands and wives have tried for years and in endless ways to change their spouse. Fact is, that person you married many years ago is pretty much going to be the same person for the duration. This is not to say that he or she won't grow in grace, but idiosyncrasies are idiosyncrasies.

Innumerable brides, who are notoriously shortsighted this side of the altar, are in love with who their fiancé could be and not who he actually is. They think they can change him. And when they change him they will be happy. When they can't, they despair.

The groom, whose love is significantly preoccupied with the physical, is in love with a myth. He assumes the romance will keep him happy. He, unlike her, hopes things don't change. But physical beauty fades over time. Romance takes different forms deep into the trenches of marriage. When the thrill of the physical subsides with the onset of children, he despairs.

Each of these perspectives is naïve and selfish. Naïve in that only God can change a heart. We are powerless in the arena of another's soul. That's God's business and to arrogantly think otherwise is tantamount to idolatry. Selfish because the change (or lack thereof) we desire in our spouse is usually aimed at ourselves and our happiness. How arrogant is it for one human being to require an adjustment in another human being for the sake of personal happiness? What's more, all the exhortations in Scripture regarding marriage confront our need for our own change and not our spouse's. We don't even live up to our own standards. How can we require others to do the same?

Our focus should not be changing our spouse, but God changing ourself. Does this mean we have to ignore areas of sin and disobedience in our spouse's life? No. But it does mean we can't blur the line between ourselves and the Holy Spirit. God may use us as an instrument to transform our spouse, but there are no guarantees. And this cannot be the reason for our obedience.

This is a serious gut check. We have to ask ourselves whether or not our desire for change in our spouse is ultimately motivated by a desire for personal happiness or for God's glory. Why exactly do we want our spouse to be different? Is what we want the same thing God wants?

BE CAREFUL WHAT YOU PRAY FOR

Countless wives pray fervently that their husbands will become the spiritual leader they ought to be. Husbands pray that wives will follow them with a willing heart. I would caution each to reconsider their prayer. I wonder if they're ready for the outcome if God should grant it.

What would happen if our spouses changed and started fulfilling their roles in our marriages? If wives relinquished control and left their husbands with the full weight of responsibility before God. What would happen to the progress of the home? Or, what if husbands actually took the keys back and began to lead? What if they made some hard decisions about finances that affected the standard of living within the home? What would happen? (We'd pray different prayers, no doubt.) Have we really thought about what we're asking for? We may want to reconsider.

Besides, marriages are not changed overnight or by the application of superficial solutions. Obviously God can bring change in the twinkling of an eye, but usually He doesn't. If you're looking for a quick fix from a book or seminar, your outlook on life is too simplistic.

The road back to God's design for marriage is paved with repentance, crosses, and the transformation of individual hearts. Many marriages are in such difficult straits the members are willing to try anything that might help. Acupuncture. Shock therapy. I understand this. Yet while there may be many helpful programs and an abundance of human advice out there, you can't place your faith in any of them.

BACK TO PREMARITAL

Our most complex issues within marriage are usually the result of fundamental failures that have festered over a long period of time. You have to climb a tree before you can fall out of it. As with most things in our Christian lives, we overcomplicate the problems and overprescribe the solutions. We make complex messes out of a relationship that has basic biblical principles at its core. Every couple that sits down to receive crisis marital counsel is really back in premarital. It's always back to the basics.

All those thorny issues that arise are merely symptoms of basic causes. An absence of humility. A negligent spiritual life. An unwillingness to die to self. A failure to obey Christ. Either these realities never sunk in, or were forgotten along the way. When it comes right down to it, the principles that are important to a marriage are central to the Christian life. Love. Sacrifice. Service.

Marriages are too often an idol. We place our faith and happiness in an ideal. The reason so many of us are so unhappy in marriage is because we have put our hope in a person other than Jesus Christ. If your happiness is dependent upon the performance of your spouse, you're destined to be disappointed. You're married to a sinner. So is she. Marriage is what happens when sinners unite.

Christ has to be the object of our faith and the priority of our love, not each other. In a real sense, we have to love Christ more than we love our spouse to actually love our spouse as we should. The level of sacrifice we're called to within marriage will seem absurd without a deep understanding of His cross and the gospel.

Here's a hard-core truth: Your responsibility within marriage is not contingent upon how well your spouse fulfills hers. But this is exactly what most people assume. "If he is not loving toward me, I do not have to be loving to him." Or "If she is not affectionate towards me, I don't have to serve her." It's at this point we see the peculiar nature of biblical love. It dies. It does not complain.

In other words, our marriages most often operate on the principle of reciprocity—good for good and bad for bad. This is conditional at best. But, in reality, what Christ has called us to is unconditional love.

The kind of love He had toward us. The gospel is dripping with grace. His love for us was not conditioned upon our love for Him. As Romans 5:8 says, "While we were yet sinners, Christ died..." *Mysteries* like these are the only *realities* that can sustain us when our love and service go unappreciated. Christ is the only one who can effectively remind us that honoring God in our marriages is *not* based on reciprocity.

How much time have you spent praying for your spouse and marriage? Most haven't prayed at all. They've just complained. Others have "prayed without ceasing." But even so, what have you prayed for? That she would stop making your life so painful? That she would wake up to your needs? That she would see the damage she is doing? Or have you prayed that she would love and honor the Lord even above you and your needs? You should. To do so frees you from the tyranny of self. It empowers your marriage by giving it a much greater goal than mere happiness.

Ironically, if you want to have a truly blessed and peaceful marriage, you cannot be the priority of it. If you and your mate are sold out in your love for the Savior, the rest will take care of itself. You want your marriage to change? Stop trying to change your spouse.

Something glorious happens when husbands and wives quit fretting over the other's failed duties and seek to fulfill theirs out of obedience to Christ. There occurs a selfless symmetry that exists in no other enterprise. The husband, inspired by his Savior's unconditional love, cherishes his wife despite her frequent resemblance to Cruella De Vil. The wife, moved by her Lord's self-sacrificing submission to the Father, quietly serves her husband despite the occasional manifestation of Archie Bunker. The husband, noticing the wife's love and honor, is drawn to her. Inexplicably, he puts her needs above his own in a desire to serve her. She, benefiting from his sacrificial service, grows in respect for him, seeking to be a help to him wherever she can. And on and on it goes until it spirals out of control and they end up on their crosses dying to self and bringing glory to His name.

10

WIVES: DON'T LIVE IN FEAR OF YOUR WIFE; LEAD HER

Let your clothes be white all the time, and let not oil be lacking on your head. Enjoy life with the woman whom you love all the days of your fleeting life which He has given to you under the sun; for this is your reward in life and in your toil in which you have labored under the sun.

{ ECCLESIASTES 9:8-9 }

Eight hours into an international flight I was attempting to recover feeling in my lower extremities. (There isn't a chair in existence with twelve hours' worth of padding.) A few reading lights were illumined in the massive fuselage, but most everyone was asleep. An enviable slumber for a man who suffers from airborne insomnia. It was a rather peaceful moment alone among 400 sleeping passengers 30,000 feet over the void at 500 miles per hour.

As I was standing near the mid bulkhead doing "plane yoga," a couple stepped out into the aisle and headed my way from the back of the sleepy plane. As they neared, I noticed that the Arabic gentleman in his mid-sixties manifested the distinctive mannerisms of Parkinson's.

My conjecture was confirmed as the man's wife supported him in his struggle to walk. They carefully managed the seams in the floor and maneuvered the occasional leg in the aisle as he reached from headrest to headrest. When they finally reached the open area in front of the restrooms, he ran out of headrests to lean upon. He then stepped into the open area only to discover that the restrooms were occupied. We stood there in silence together as they waited.

At some point, he lost his balance and instinctually reached for me to steady himself. I reached right back. From his chronic hunch he looked up at me with grateful eyes. His wife nodded and smiled a "Thank you."

The three strangers remained in each other's grasp for about five minutes adjusting in unison to the intermittent bumps of altitude. Not a word was exchanged. Personally, I was speechless—never having been so close to such sacrificial love. It was a sight to behold. I wondered what my own marriage looked like in the eyes of others. What do they see in our eyes as we look at each other?

Apparently the two gents occupying the toilets had decided to shower, shave, bake a cake, balance their checkbooks, and write their memoirs. After what seemed like forever, one of them emerged. My friend bid me *adieu* and shuffled forward against the wall.

RESPECT INCARNATE

Already inspired, I was not prepared for what happened next. Unexpectedly, his wife entered the bathroom with him. Obviously, because of his broken physical condition, she had to. I broke into tears at the sight of it. (There are tears in my eyes even now as I recount this event.) Such grace and love. Despite the context, it was an extraordinarily dignified moment. Compassion covers shame. I was overwhelmed by the meekness of his condition and the selflessness of hers.

There's no way to describe the depth of the sincerity I saw in her eyes when she looked at her husband. She cared deeply for his dignity. She was an adornment to her husband's life. Every man wants his wife to look at him that way. I had one thought: *I pray my wife will love me enough to take me to the bathroom…when I'm old.* It was respect incarnate.

With tears in my eyes I returned to my seat, woke my wife, and asked, "Will you love me enough to take me to the bathroom when I'm old?" (The look on her face was priceless.)

Most husbands don't even notice when the look is gone. Like when a missed button on your shirt goes unnoticed until someone points it out. Almost always, the husband is the last one to get it. One day a buddy leans over during lunch and quietly lands the message, "Dude, your wife is wearing the pants." He denies it with a grunt and a shrug, but knows it's true. Everyone knows it. Somewhere, somehow, slowly over a period of days, months, years, and incalculable little instances, he handed them over.

When I first encounter such a couple I always wonder what the real story is. Believe me, there is always a story. On the outside, they look like the couple that "comes with the frame." I once put a lot of faith in those images. I'd get excited when well-groomed families showed up at church. Alternatively, I'd get nervous when others—apparently having just stepped off the set of Jerry Springer—plopped their desperation down in our pews. Now I have the opposite reactions. The former usually have a disaster of suburban proportions lurking beneath their perfect smiles. Whereas the latter are beyond hiding stuff and are broken enough to ask for help. The former couples deal in pretentious overtures. The latter deal in truth.

If the husband were being transparent he'd tell you he feels more like her oldest child than her husband. He pouts like a child when he doesn't get sex. He retreats in defensiveness when she questions his decisions. He clams up when it comes time to talk. He avoids the inevitable conflict by deferring on all decisions, or not making them. He hides from the rigors of success in the weeds of mediocrity. A mere boy dragging around a grown man's carcass.

Truly, she's more like a nanny than a wife. She grew up at the birth of her children. He never did. These guys are a dime a dozen. You can see them coming from a mile away, as they too have their own distinct mannerisms—lifelessness and timidity.

What stings him most is the lack of respect. Mind you, it's not always an overt disrespect. Then again, sometimes it is. I've witnessed wives who flat out belittle their husbands in public. It's disheartening. But for most couples it's not explicit. It's subtle. It's the pervasive absence of honor radiating from her person. It's the reality that she respects other men—pastors, coaches, physicians, Dr. Oz—more than she respects him. She turns to them for guidance and counsel while barely trusting him with the time of day. In all this, the only person more miserable than him…is her.

There's a world of resentment in her eyes, not respect. They tell a thousand stories about his failures, inadequacies, and incompetence. Her closest friends have heard them all.

ONE PRECIOUS DROP AT A TIME

There are few experiences (I can think of some) more exhilarating to the soul of a man than to see respect in his wife's eyes. It's like jet fuel for the male psyche. Not a romanticized image of a wife who calls her husband "lord" and swoons at his every arrival. I mean a wife who trusts her husband with her life. Looks to him above all others and *wants* to follow him. That's respect.

Respect is a depletable resource. As a husband, you only get so much to start. It comes with the position and is downloaded at the altar. Any reserve is earned over time. What you have has to be protected. Once it's gone, it's hard to get back. Sometimes never. Most men waste it one negligent drop at a time. An unfulfilled commitment. A broken promise. A missed duty. A harsh word. Eventually, she doesn't have an ounce of respect for him.

There's a debate over which comes first—the weak husband or the controlling wife. Not much unlike the biblical resolution to the chicken or the egg dilemma, the answer is obvious—the (chicken) husband. Granted, this isn't always the case, but more often than not the blame lies with him.

Sometimes the cause is obvious—catastrophic failure on the husband's part. Adultery. Financial ruin. Pornography. Most times it's more subtle—a gradual negligence of his responsibilities over time.

Other times her disposition contributes to the mess. Maybe she inherited a diminished view of men from dear old mom or was negatively affected by the constant punch line regarding men delivered by the culture. Regardless, if a husband is willing to hand over the keys, the wife will gladly take them up. It's in the male DNA to neglect his responsibility. It's in the female DNA to want it.

Whether husbands realize it or not, their greatest fear is their duty. It's a fear that absolutely controls some men. They know how much sacrifice is required and how much hangs in the balance with each decision. It's a weird insecurity that causes men to withdraw from their primary responsibility—leadership.

In many instances, all their juvenile irresponsibility results from the prospect of failure and the sting of her potential disappointment. It can be terrifying. Rather than humbling himself—acknowledging his shortcomings—and doing what he's called to do, he crawls into a cave of insecurity. Once that happens, it's hard to coax him out.

IT'S DOWN TO ONE QUESTION

Here's a typical scenario. A frustrated wife comes to see me and says something along these lines: "I want my husband to lead, and I ask him to do so all the time." Usually I laugh out loud. Usually I'm the only one who sees the humor. Usually my response creates an awkward moment. But I'm not mocking the wife. I'm agreeing with her. It's so predictable.

I can almost retell their story without knowing it. I describe scenarios that capture her feelings almost exactly. She's asking for counsel because she does not want to carry the family anymore. She wants a leader to rise up out of the couch. Then I ask the ultimate question: "Do you respect your husband?" She immediately realizes its significance and pleads the Fifth: "I don't know." Basically, I have my answer.

So as not to be harpooned by political correctness, egalitarians, and angry wives everywhere, let me be clear. I'm not painting the husband as a victim and the wife as the villain. I'm not stereotyping women as shallow and irrational people who throw fits or threaten temporary abstinence if they don't get their way. Usually the wife is far more competent in far more areas. What I'm saying is that her frustration is most often a result of the husband's unwillingness and not her desire for control.

The confusion of roles started with her husband. He put her in this position. He may resent her opinion of him, but he formed it.

Ironically, this dude's basic motive in neglecting his responsibilities is selfish—*self-preservation*. Rather than lead, he abandons leadership to ensure his own comfort. You couldn't make him grow up if you tried. And she has. He's afraid to. He's concerned about the many deficiencies in his character that would be exposed should he undertake his role.

GRABBING FOR THE WHEEL

Can you imagine what it must be like for wives? They're in a far more difficult position than the husband. Especially if she has a sincere desire to honor God as a wife. What's a wife to do? Having to trust their lives to such imperfect instruments has to be scary. It reminds me of driving instructors who intentionally put themselves in the passenger seat with vastly inexperienced drivers behind the wheel. Wives can suffer from ditch to ditch for decades. No wonder they so often grab for the wheel.

Insecure husbands force their wives to resort to various and subtle forms of counterintelligence in order to advance the household. Otherwise, if she's direct, he overreacts in defensiveness. She lives in the land of eggshells. Passive aggressiveness is a telltale sign. "My, the garbage can is full!" instead of "Will you put down the game controller and please take the garbage out?" All the time she's begging him to join her in the enterprise of the family. She's desperately trying to put the keys back in his hand. The wife's been left with the impossible task of finishing his dad's job—raising a man.

YOU CAN SEE IT COMING FROM MILES AWAY

The signs were there back in premarital. If you know what to look for, you can see them. When I ask men in premarital to define the leadership of the husband they most always get it wrong. They throw in a few noble sounding words like *provide* and *protect*, but they haven't the slightest idea what's entailed. Most often they have only one thing on their mind. You ask, "Do you think you are ready to lead this young woman?" He wonders, *When can we start having sex?*

Most of these precious young women naïvely end up marrying

boys. It's a bait and switch. She'll ignore almost anything to get the invitations out. He'll say almost anything to get to the honeymoon. The solemn responsibility of caring for her soul never occurs to him until he realizes the garbage won't take itself out.

Women don't respect men who are afraid of their duty or are too lazy to undertake it. They tolerate them. Ultimately you cannot live in fear of your wife and truly love her. You can't live in fear of your duty and love her either.

Many wives get nervous at this very point. They assume the alternative is the opposite of passivity, tyranny. Certainly many men are despots who almost completely ignore the feelings or needs of the wife. This too is a dreadful misunderstanding of the gospel (and a different chapter).

The true alternative is the glory of God. You must fear God in view of your responsibility to love and lead your wife as you should. Wives respect men who fear God more than they fear their wives. What a wife wants to know is that her husband is controlled by transcendent realties, not fleeting or selfish ones. It's what she needs. It's the best love a husband can offer, because it's always in her best interest. Honestly, she wants to know that when it comes right down to it the question is not "What would make her happy?" or "What does she prefer?" but "What does God desire?" The rest takes care of itself.

There will come times when your role as leader will require you to make decisions that scare the both of you. The out-of-state job opportunity away from mom and dad that could greatly improve your family's future. The decision to lower your standard of living to better honor the Lord with your finances. All kinds of decisions will have to be negotiated and discussed. The two of you will not always agree. You will not always make the right choice. But if your wife respects you, she will trust you. If she respects you, you will see it in her eyes.

> Husbands ought also to love their own wives as their own
> bodies. He who loves his own wife loves himself; for no
> one ever hated his own flesh, but nourishes and cherishes it,
> just as Christ also does the church, because we are members
> of His body. For this reason a man shall leave his father and
> mother, and shall be joined to his wife, and the two shall

become one flesh. This mystery is great; but I am speaking with reference to Christ and the church. Nevertheless, each individual among you also is to love his own wife even as himself; and the wife must see to it that she respect her husband (Ephesians 5:28-33).

11

SIN: DIE TO SELF UPSIDE DOWN

*It is a trustworthy statement, deserving full acceptance, that Christ
Jesus came into the world to save sinners, among whom I am
foremost of all. Yet for this reason I found mercy, so that in me as
the foremost, Jesus Christ might demonstrate His perfect patience
as an example for those who would believe in Him for eternal life.*

{ 1 TIMOTHY 1:15-16 }

You know that moment when "icicles are hanging on the banisters" and the two of you are lying back to back in bed—*seething*. (Don't know what I'm talking about? Whatever. You're not married yet? Buckle up!) Inevitably the first thing that comes to mind is the absurdity of the situation. It's most always about nothing—chicken recipes, toilet seats, socks, etc. No one can ever finally trace their origin; arguments just happen. They spontaneously self-generate out of nonsense. And once they do, there's no going back. We're all in. Why is it the last thing that comes to mind is saying, "I'm sorry"? We're a stubborn race. Especially when it comes to admitting wrong. We've been blowing it since the beginning of time. Yet it's always someone else's fault. Wives, snakes, dads, Little Debbie, anyone but self.

At that moment, it's a short distance from one restless soul to the other, but it's a hundred miles from pride to pride. We roll the echo of painful words around in our head like a sore tooth we can't keep our tongue off. In the instant replay of our mind we never lose those arguments. We're always the victors. So, we wait until the loser breaks and acquiesces to our terms of surrender.

As we wait for their confession, deep within a nagging contradiction bores its way into our conscience. *How can one forgiven sinner withhold forgiveness from the other? How can I act so cruelly toward the person I love more than any other?*

> Let all bitterness and wrath and anger and clamor and slander be put away from you, along with all malice. Be kind to one another, tender-hearted, forgiving each other, just as God in Christ also has forgiven you (Ephesians 4:31-32).

How stupid we must look from heaven. From up there all our spats come down to that one timeless and indefensible polemic: "I know you are, but what am I?" Stupid humans.

Eventually there emerges in us a rivalry between competing desires—the want to reach out and a resistance to reconciliation. This battle is about as face-to-face as we'll ever get to the darkness of our sinfulness. We are tenaciously selfish people at our core. It is the immovable force of pride coming into the space of the irresistible power of God's grace. God is the only strength known to man that can change him. The longer we reflect, the more surrender appears reasonable. Trust me, that's not our natural inclination, but a divine one. Which is why we resist it for so long.

Finally, we roll over, reach out to touch the sobbing silhouette opposite us, and say, "Honey, I'm a jerk. I'm sorry for what I said. My mom's chicken is not better than yours. That was so stupid of me." She rolls over with tears and says, "Me too." The rest is legendary.

GET HERE SOON

But, it takes so long to get here. We're as quick to harden as we are to break. Looking inward will never be our gut reaction. Reaching out for forgiveness is always someone else's responsibility.

There is nothing about yielding that appeals to the battle-ready human heart, especially the male version. It's about as counterintuitive an idea as is possible for a fallen human being to conceive. Self-preservation is an involuntary muscle and defensiveness is our resting heart rate. Pride covers our conscience and won't let us see the truth about who we are. Trust me, it's dark in there.

When Paul begged the question of self-effacement with the proud Corinthians, "Why not be wronged? Why not be defrauded?" they probably giggled. It did not register. Then they realized, "Oh, he's serious."

> Actually, then, it is already a defeat for you, that you have lawsuits with one another. Why not rather be wronged? Why not rather be defrauded? On the contrary, you yourselves wrong and defraud. You do this even to your brethren.
>
> Or do you not know that the unrighteous will not inherit the kingdom of God? Do not be deceived; neither fornicators, nor idolaters, nor adulterers, nor effeminate, nor homosexuals, nor thieves, nor the covetous, nor drunkards, nor revilers, nor swindlers, will inherit the kingdom of God. Such were some of you; but you were washed, but you were sanctified, but you were justified in the name of the Lord Jesus Christ and in the Spirit of our God (1 Corinthians 6:7-11).

Undoubtedly, the Corinthians were at the ready with six dozen reasonable answers to Paul's questions. "Because I have rights." "Because it's unfair." "Because it's painful." "Because they deserve to pay for what they did." Obviously the Corinthians realized the excruciating implication of Paul's suggestion—death to self. Even if someone wrongs you, is it necessary to defend self? Must you retaliate? Can't you let it go? The implied answer is hard to stomach. Only Jesus makes the yes make sense. These questions pick at the core of our struggle. We bristle.

The great evangelist George Whitefield once received a letter in which he was brutally criticized by a peer. He was called everything but a preacher. Whitefield, with impeccable clarity, penned the best response to criticism I've ever encountered. He wrote his assassin a brief reply: "Thank you sir for your criticism. If you knew about me what I know about me, you would have written a longer letter." Genius. Whitefield got it. *We all deserve longer letters.* If we can ever get here in our hearts, the world will open up to us. The gospel says, "Get here soon."

Our self-portraits lack this type of realism. Our depictions are way too respectable. We've penned sonnets and deserve requiems. We've been conditioned to hedge on who we really are and deflect the truth about us.

HOUSES ON FIRE AND SMILES ON FACES

Our problem not only shows itself in our many interpersonal conflicts, but also lies at the base of our chronic failures. Like the self-respecting Corinthians, we can offer up dozens of "reasonable" answers for why we are the way we are. None of them even comes close to explaining us and all of them are pretty much the same—*we're victims.*

When our finances end up in shambles we tell people, "I just can't catch a break." The real story is our decades-long refusal to live within our means. Our checkbook tells the truth, but no one's getting near it.

When we bounce from job to job we blame our bosses. "I can't work for that guy." The truth is we've no work ethic, or we've vastly overestimated our personal value. Instead of getting off our cans we fall upon "brilliant" business ideas. "I'll start a silk-screening business in my garage. Once I move the exercise equipment, I'll get started."

When our wives take over the house we say, "She's a control freak." What actually happened was a slow abdication of our leadership through persistent negligence. She has to control everything, or there would be nothing to control.

When innumerable small tasks around the house remain unfinished we say, "I'm so busy" or "I've got ADHD." Really? Actually, what we have is a serious case of the don'ts. We *don't* want to do what we're supposed to. We're lazy and unorganized.

When we're fifty pounds overweight and can't run a mile without calling paramedics we say, "It's my metabolism" or "I'm carbohydrate sensitive." The truth is our untamed appetites have us pinned to the couch. Taking drastic measures, we cut back on calories. Regular Oreos instead of double-stuffed. Marketing defibrillators for domestic and institutional use actually was a "brilliant" idea. No doubt the wife of a middle-age man came up with it.

From time to time, friends sit us down and try to get to the "thing" underneath. They struggle with words. It's awkward. They ask, "How are things?" We answer, "Oh, fine. Things are really good." Not reacting to the stunned look on their face is a learned skill.

Our entire house is engulfed in flames behind us and we smile. They scream, "Dude! Your house is burning down!" We calmly reply, "Yeah. It's a beautiful shade of orange, isn't it? We're gonna toast marshmallows later." If we would ever focus the energy and time we waste trying to hide things from others and apply it to changing ourselves, we just might get results.

THE CROSS RATS US OUT

It's so hard to rat ourselves out. "It's me. I'm the way I am because of me. I'm a sinner. I hate discipline. It's my fault. I'm discontent. I'm a failure as a husband. I've mailed it in for years. I love Little Debbie and all her products." As hard as it is to understand, there's unequalled freedom in a brutally honest self-appraisal. Whitefield was on to something. Death to self presents us with a liberty that comes only from the gospel and the cross.

The cross simultaneously declares two indispensable realities. First, it proclaims the unbelievable news about the grace of God. God loves sinners and sent His Son to redeem them. It is unconditional and radical love on display. Every time we behold it we rejoice. Second, the cross communicates the most brutal assessment of man's condition we will ever face. We're worse than we let on. We'll never be as honest about ourselves as the cross is.

The cross tells us straight up that we are vicious rebels who deserve a vicious death. If you believe Jesus died for you, you already hold this. Did Jesus deserve such a horrible death? No. Well then who did? "Me! That's my death!" we declare. At the cross we reach out for the truth. We're worse than we can imagine. Why else would Christ die? Every time we consider this reality we rejoice in the first one.

To truly appreciate the gospel, we must come to terms with who we are. The more we face the sinfulness of our heart, the more we will relish grace. At the core of all our unresolved conflicts and dishonesty about who we are lies an unwillingness to admit what the cross is screaming. Deep down, we're messed up. All our superficial explanations don't even get close to the truth. The smell of our "smoke" rises above them all. The mishaps on the surface of our life are the symptoms of the real problems below.

When we face the truth of the cross head on, it makes our self-preservation appear foolish. The person who defends self when God gave Himself to save us from His wrath doesn't understand grace. The man who offers excuses for his sin when God offered His Son to pay for it has no real apprehension of the gospel. The individual who diminishes the offense of his sin before others also treats the cross like a poignant gesture of a well-meaning God. The man who won't admit the truth about his life can't truly enjoy the benefits of Christ's. None of this will makes sense unless the cross is in view.

But, we can come clean. What Jesus has done for us on the cross relieves us of the need to defend self. Clearly, there's nothing worth defending. We no longer have to offer excuses because Jesus has dealt with all our failures. There are no real excuses anyway. We don't have to dodge the severity of our sin because He forgave it. To acknowledge this draws more attention to His grace than it does to our sin. I can tell people the hard truth about my actions because they already know. Most importantly, God was aware of all my sin when He redeemed me. It's what He saved me from.

Once you get here, you'll know true freedom. You won't be imprisoned by the need to defend, or to be thought well of by men. You'll always write longer letters than they write. Long before you go to bed angry you'll apologize to your wife because to do so jeopardizes nothing. You're already her servant.

You will allow people to speak into your life without qualifying every word they say. You'll be open to criticism without being defensive. You'll accept help and admit defeat. Insecurities—which are our nervous efforts to keep the truth about us away from other people— meet their match in Jesus, who knew the truth and died for us anyway.

STEALING THE GIFTS AT OUR PARTY

When we're insecure it's as if we're attempting to cover up that which God uncovered on the cross and finally dealt with. To deny the cross is like stealing our gifts at our own party. Why not just enjoy what's been given to us—righteousness? We don't have to live that way anymore.

The world says a man who admits wrong and gives in to criticism is weak. I expect the world to say that. Stupid humans. Masculinity, according to the culture, is the ability to defend self, control others, and seek revenge. But power, according to Christ, is being above defensiveness and excuses. A total self-control.

Freedom is the ability to look at ourselves before we seek to blame others. Christ-centered masculinity is having the strength to face criticism even when it's wrong and simultaneously remember that we deserve worse. The first thing that comes to mind to those hanging on crosses is the absence of power and rights.

Peter, that boisterous and loud "man's man" who did all he could to impress Christ and gain a leg up on his peers, had the truth of real power crash in around him during the garden raid. When Jesus refused to reach for His sword in self-defense and Peter had already lopped off someone's ear with his, he knew the truth about Christ and himself. At the moment he was running from the startling reality of the cross.

> Jesus said to him, "Put your sword back into its place; for all those who take up the sword shall perish by the sword. Or do you think that I cannot appeal to My Father, and He will at once put at My disposal more than twelve legions of angels? How then will the Scriptures be fulfilled, which say that it must happen this way?" (Matthew 26:52-54).

Peter's encounter with real strength eventually transformed him into a humble, useful vessel of grace. As tradition goes, by the end of his life, self-sacrifice seemed so reasonable a response to the person of Christ that he asked to be crucified upside down in order to honor his Lord. Freedom.

Would that we could die to self upside down every day. Men who learn the habit are real men indeed. They make extraordinary leaders.

Fearlessly, they do the right thing in spite of consequences. Rarely do they take into consideration the perception of others when carrying out their tasks. Armed with clear consciences, they receive criticism with barely a whimper. They love to learn of their blind spots so they can make themselves more invisible than they already are. They do right by those they lead, having their best interests in mind at all times. They don't micromanage enterprises into oblivion out of a need to be recognized as in charge. They give power away; they don't hoard it.

WHAT FREEDOM CAN DO TO A MAN

He is a good father. Knowing his own sin, he has compassion on the little creatures under his care. It really does hurt him more than it hurts them. More than once he's humbled himself and admitted failure to his own children. When they struggle against the challenges of adolescence and self-discovery he does not abandon them, but sympathizes. How could it be otherwise when he himself is still struggling by grace? He runs beside their lives until they have the balance to take it on their own.

He is a slightly above average husband. Bound by the cross of Christ, he cherishes his wife despite all her foibles. In the same way Christ loved him. He's a realist who understands sin's effect on the human heart. He offers forgiveness instead of condemnation. The authority bestowed on him as the head of the home hasn't inclined him to despotism but servanthood. He knows he's not good at everything and feels no insecure need to pretend. He acknowledges his limitations and depends on his wife's gifts and talents to make up the difference. He's secure enough to allow her to shine. He's sacrificial and defers because he can. He reaches out in the midst of their ridiculous arguments and asks forgiveness before she has to. He eats her chicken and—even though it's horrible—says, "I've never tasted chicken quite like this before."

MAN LAWS

1. You may never refer to your clothing as an outfit.

2. You should avoid all "sports" that require you to point your toe before starting, or if they include "routines" or "elements."

3. You may never use another man's lip balm. The only exceptions are being lost in a desert, caught in a blizzard, or trapped in an avalanche. Each scenario still requires you to trim off the top layer with a pocketknife. You must apply it with same pocketknife.

4. Two men may never use the same umbrella no matter how hard it is raining.

5. You must check your nails only by making a fist in front of your face. Never do so by way of "jazz fingers."

6. You must check something on your shoes only by lifting up your heel in front of you. Never do so by looking behind you in the "ballerina pose."

7. You can never know the lyrics or recognize the melodies to any songs by Taylor Swift or Miley Cyrus. I don't actually know who these people are. I've only been warned myself.

8. Celine Deon, Kenny G, and Josh Groban cannot be discovered on your iPod.

9. You must never admit to never having viewed the Bourne trilogy.

10. You must be able to locate (at all times) the duct tape in your house when asked.

11. You must agree to attend all air shows or car shows when invited by friends.

12. There are no "points" in baseball.

13. There is no such thing as capris for men.

14. If a man's fly is unzipped, he's on his own.

15. One space is required between each urinal in use.

16. You may never brag about the features in your wife's minivan.

17. You must be able to throw a spiral. You must know what this is.

18. You must never watch ice skating or men's gymnastics.

19. You may never choose between Jack Bauer and Jason Bourne.

20. You can make no more than one adjustment when parallel parking. If you need more, circle the block.

21. A head nod suffices when greeting another man.

22. No one ever "hurts your feelings."

23. You must stop on a given station whenever Boston's "More Than a Feeling" is playing.

24. You must be able to perform a perfect air drum solo when listening to Rush's "Tom Sawyer."

25. "Shotgun" can only be called when the car is in view.

26. Never trot in public. Sprint or walk only. (Jogging for exercise not applicable.)

27. If available, the bone-in rib eye is always the correct choice.

28. If you have a cat you cannot have feelings for it.

29. The Labrador retriever is always the default dog.

30. You cannot own dogs that can be mistaken for throw pillows.

31. You cannot talk to your pets in "baby" or "sweet talk" voices.

32. You can never be a passenger on a motorcycle with another man. Walk. No matter how far the destination is.

33. Never use rolling backpacks.

34. It's a man purse even if you refer to it as a European courier bag.

35. Men may not be in a revolving door together.

36. You must shout "Play ball!" at the end of the national anthem regardless of the occasion at which it is played. This includes funerals.

37. No dead fish handshakes.

38. It is okay to weep at the sight of fighter jets flying over a stadium during the national anthem.

39. Joe Montana is the best quarterback of all time.

40. You must argue about 39.

12

SEX: IT IS NOT EVIL

*You have made my heart beat faster, my sister, my bride; you
have made my heart beat faster with a single glance of your
eyes, with a single strand of your necklace. How beautiful is your
love, my sister, my bride! How much better is your love than
wine, and the fragrance of your oils than all kinds of spices!*

{ SONG OF SOLOMON 4:9-10 }

W hen do you know it's time to talk to your children about sex?"
Q&As are risky formats. This question came after I delivered
a lecture on biblical sexuality. Given the topic you'd think I would
have been prepared for it. But I wasn't. I stumbled over my words
and formulated some sort of answer laced with *perhaps* and *maybe.*
One of those responses preachers offer when they have no idea what
they're talking about. It sounds profound, but when the smoke clears
it's meaningless. I'd have been better off saying, "I don't know." But
who'd ever risk saying that? "Next question!"

Here's what I do know. By the time most parents get around to
asking the question, they're way behind schedule. Reacting and not
planning. In some inexplicable way, the irrefutable and very predictable biological realities sneak up on them. As if the physical and emotional changes emerged overnight. "Dear? Why does Johnny smell like
cologne?"

Adolescence is the biggest heads-up of all time. When most parents
step back from their careers and schedules long enough to notice the
changes, or dads get up the courage to broach the subject, their sons
know far more than they imagine. If you choose to remain silent, the

121

world steps in with an explicit crash course on the pleasures of instant gratification.

Face it—there are certain awkward conversations that have to take place. If we care at all, we'll swallow our pride and have them. Up first—the legendary anatomy and physiology lecture. Innocence lost. Your son never looks at females the same. Then—if you're courageous enough—there's the masturbation speech. "We need to talk." Your son loses consciousness from embarrassment. Then there's the highly specialized conversation prior to the honeymoon night. "It's not like you've seen on TV. Lower your expectations. Don't be a Sasquatch." Your son (and daughter-in-law) will thank you for this one.

But these are merely individual—generally helpful—speeches. The sum of these patented lectures isn't the same as *guiding* your son through the minefield of sexuality. If the above conversations are the extent of the counsel you've provided, your son is in trouble. It's about as much as he could hope to find in a biology class or men's locker room. There's so much more to the subject than physiology. Which brings me to the answer I now have cued up.

It's not one conversation. It's multiple conversations. And, it's not only about sex. It's about the truths that make sex make sense—God, creation, Christ, the gospel, and the purpose for marriage. It's countless conversations about life lived in light of the cross and how God intended life to be. How Christianity—rooted in the gospel—makes everything clear, even sex. It's the truth about the culture's definition and estimation of sex—which is among the biggest deceptions of all time. It's the presentation of a biblical worldview, which includes a proper understanding of sex.

Most Christian couples struggle to maintain a biblical point of view on the subject. You'd be surprised to know how many "healthy" couples struggle in this area. The odds are stacked against us. For one, we're born perverted. What was the first thing our original parents did when they sinned? Hide and cover their loins. Should we be surprised the rest of humanity so far removed from their innocence is confused sexually? We're messed up from the start. Such is the reason the apostle was so direct in 1 Corinthians:

> Now concerning the things about which you wrote, it is
> good for a man not to touch a woman. But because of
> immoralities, each man is to have his own wife, and each
> woman is to have her own husband. The husband must
> fulfill his duty to his wife, and likewise also the wife to her
> husband (7:1-3).

In addition, there's little discipleship available on the subject. Couples head into marriage with little or no clarity. Most Christian men haven't figured it out even after decades of sex within the biblical union of marriage. We're still discovering what a healthy sexual relationship is years into it. If this is true, why would we assume a teenage boy could figure it out on his own? But we do.

GOOD LUCK, JOHNNY! REMEMBER TO STOP!

Usually dads spend more time teaching their sons about how to ride a bike than they do about the most intimate physical/spiritual relationship they'll ever experience. Seriously. When I taught my sons how to ride a bike, I was careful. Helmets. Pads. Planned the route. Due to the potential dangers, I ran beside them for miles until they found their balance.

We do not take our son to the tallest hill we can find, perched just above a busy intersection, then stand downhill next to a stop sign, and yell, "Start pedaling, Johnny! Remember to stop!" That would be stupid. We'd be reported to child protection services. Yet when it comes to sex, something that has a similar potential for destruction, this is exactly what we do. "Good luck, son! Hope you get the hang of it." Eventually he takes a header into the oncoming traffic of the culture. The negligence here is mind-boggling.

The church has been complicit in the negligence. Recently we've made greater efforts to fill the vacuum left by our silence. More sermons, seminars, and books are written on the subject than ever before. In some cases, it's very helpful information. In other cases, we look foolish. This happens every time the church mimics the world.

The now infamous "Seven Days of Sex" campaign is a perfect

example. Couples were commissioned by their pastor to have sex every day for one week. Besides ecstatic husbands, I have no idea what this accomplished. The apparent logic? More sex leads to happiness. Great! Go ahead and propagate the same message as pornography, but do it in the name of Christ. Not surprisingly, this same preacher brought a bed up on stage as a prop and had his wife sit on it while he talked about their sex life. Nothing like demeaning your wife in front of thousands of men. What he offered was more like a Monty Python skit than a biblical illustration.

The Bible's perspective is the exact opposite of culture's—a deeper spiritual union between husband and wife *leads* to a genuine physical relationship. Not the other way around.

Generally, most churches have no strategy for helping disciple their young men in this area, or helping fathers mentor their sons. (That is, until your marriage is in crisis mode due to an affair or an exposed addiction to pornography. Then we're happy to tell you everything we should have told you twenty years ago.) What do most young Christian men hear from the church about sex? Sex is evil and never to be mentioned among decent people.

Basically, the church's response is the exact opposite of the world's. But it's also damaging. The world so overexposes the subject that it's devalued down to the level of a primordial instinct. It's about gratification, dominance, and physical pleasure. Women are viewed as recreational equipment.

On the other side, the church so avoids the subject that sex becomes taboo. Young men are conditioned to be ashamed of the very feelings God intended them to have. As a result, they enter into their high school and college years caught between the extremes of overt promiscuity and secret struggles with lust. It's utterly confusing.

I once had a newly married couple confess feelings of guilt for having had sex on Sunday. I'm serious. It was hard not to laugh out loud. Eventually I was able to dispel their superstition. This type of nonsense pretty much sums up the church's message on sex: It's bad.

One author aptly described the takeaway from evangelical Christianity on the subject of sex as "Moral people are less sexual." But sex is not evil. Not even on Sundays. After all, God created it. Furthermore, sex is not something of which we should be ashamed. Again, not even on Sundays.

MORAL PEOPLE ENJOY SEX

The desire for sex is not immoral. Believe it or not, even moral people enjoy sex. The desire is a normal part of God's design for men and women within marriage. God commanded husbands and wives to have sex when He commanded them to procreate. What's more, He designed it to be uniquely pleasurable. Which is His grace in action, since He did not have to do that. This may be hard for some Christians to comprehend, but the joy of sex is part of God's blessing.

Young men are not the only ones affected by the church's uncertainty. By the time "churched" young ladies reach marriage they've been conditioned to view sex as an obligation. Sex—they are taught—is more important to the husband. Men have a greater desire for the physical stimulation found in sex. For the wife, sex becomes somewhat of a secondary inconvenience and white-knuckle duty. The operational assumption is that men are *less* emotional and *more* physical creatures. So wives grudgingly fulfill their duty.

The damage done by this perspective is vast. For one, it causes wives to grow bitter from feeling as if they're merely pieces of meat. As a result, wives withhold sex from their husbands, or coldly participate in it. The husband, in return, withdraws from any meaningful communication with his wife and retreats to the "garage" of his mind. Which ends up verifying the wife's initial suspicion. Round and round it goes. By the time the cycle's complete, the couple ends up becoming a self-fulfilling prophecy plopped down in front of a counselor charged with deconstructing the confusion during the husband's lunch break.

SAVED FROM THE PERIL ON BOTH SIDES

The biblical perspective saves us from the extremes of both the world and the church. God intended sex to be a deeply spiritual (selfless) act and not a self-indulgent one. The culture can't get this and the church rarely gets it right. In a way that is purely Christian, the physical pleasure a person receives in sex results from the simultaneous service rendered by husband and wife toward one another in the same act of intimacy. Only a Christ-centered union can know this. The apostle went on to put it this way:

> The wife does not have authority over her own body, but the husband does; and likewise also the husband does not have authority over his own body, but the wife does. Stop depriving one another, except by agreement for a time, so that you may devote yourselves to prayer, and come together again so that Satan will not tempt you because of your lack of self-control (1 Corinthians 7:4-5).

GRACE WHEN THE THRILL IS GONE

Too many young couples enter marriage with physical attraction as the *primary* basis and motivation for marriage. Now, obviously, we don't go looking for the ugliest person we can find, but there has to be more to a marriage than physical beauty. While sex is important and should not be prudishly marginalized, it's not the enduring power of solid marriages. To think so is naïve.

Physical beauty doesn't last. If you love your wife because of her appearance, your love is conditional. If you engage her in conversation only because it might lead to sex, then your love is conditional. What happens to your love when beauty wanes? What happens when the youthful thrill of sex wears off with time and age? Both take away youthful beauty and leave us with the stark realities of life.

By itself, physical pleasure as a motivation within marriage is purely selfish. Such a motivation makes one's own physical needs the primary goal of the marital union. This perspective does not take into account the greater biblical design for marriage.

What sons really need to know is that fulfilling sex—as God intended it—*results* from a consistently sacrificial relationship built on the principle of unconditional love. "Good" sex does not *lead* to sound marriages. To leave the spiritual realities out of the sexual relationship will only lead to frustration, confusion, and selfishness. Wives will feel used in the absence of a husband's dedicated love and sensitivity. Husbands forced to beg and plead for intimacy will eventually become angry. The cross has to be central to avoid this outcome.

Sex cannot provide the type of fulfillment we imagine anyway. Only sacrificial love can. Sex is certainly part of it, but it's not all of it. When a marriage is fueled by an awareness of God's grace toward sinners, a selflessness results that sets individuals free to enjoy sex in the way God intended.

13

PORNOGRAPHY:
HUGH HEFNER WILL DIE ALONE

The lips of an adulteress drip honey and smoother than oil is her speech;
but in the end she is bitter as wormwood, sharp as a two-edged sword. Her
feet go down to death, her steps lay hold of Sheol. She does not ponder
the path of life; her ways are unstable, she does not know it. Now then,
my sons, listen to me and do not depart from the words of my mouth.
Keep your way far from her, and do not go near the door of her house.

{ PROVERBS 5:3-8 }

The commandment is a lamp and the teaching is light; and reproofs for
discipline are the way of life to keep you from the evil woman, from
the smooth tongue of the adulteress. Do not desire her beauty in your
heart, nor let her capture you with her eyelids. For on account of a
harlot one is reduced to a loaf of bread, and an adulteress hunts for the
precious life. Can a man take fire in his bosom and his clothes not be
burned? Or can a man walk on hot coals and his feet not be scorched?

{ PROVERBS 6:23-28 }

At the window of my house I looked out through my lattice, and
I saw among the naïve, and discerned among the youths a
young man lacking sense, passing through the street near her
corner; and he takes the way to her house, in the twilight, in
the evening, in the middle of the night and in the darkness.

{ PROVERBS 7:6-9 }

I magine an axe. A two-pound, four-inch red blade sharpened to a
razor's edge fastened to the end of a twenty-five-inch-long hick-
ory handle. You know the one—Paul Bunyanesque. Now imagine the

only time you've ever seen an axe like this was in horror films. Not the black-and-white Hitchcock classics, but those despicable slasher kinds where raging psychopaths mutilate and dismember their victims.

(Okay. No reasonable parents would let young kids watch horror films of this sort. But, in this scenario they do and it's perfectly normal. This is imaginary. It's also the only way this analogy works. So relax and go with it.)

If this scenario were actually true, it would be virtually impossible to have any other impression except that axes were invented for purposes of destruction and horror. Axes are dreadful. Torn flesh. Severed limbs. They're pure evil and no decent person owns one.

Then one summer you visit your grandparents' farm. On a given afternoon you come around the side of the barn to see your grandfather with an axe raised above his head. In horror you watch as your grandfather heaves it downward, laying waste to…a piece of wood? *What? Wait a minute!* There beneath his feet is a freshly massacred pile of lumber. *Isn't firewood good and useful?* you think to yourself. Yes it is. As a matter of fact, this particular firewood will eventually be placed in the potbellied stove on which your grandmother will make her incomparably delicious stew. Then the truth hits you—axes are good.

Axes, as it turns out, are not intended for harm at all. This is not to suggest they can't cause harm, but that is not the purpose of axes. The impression you've been given is completely wrong. Axes are actually very helpful. They are centuries-old tools essential to the existence of people in more primitive and rustic contexts.

Though dangerous, they're designed with noble purposes in mind. It's the psychopaths who pervert the nature of axes and use them for depraved ends. In the wrong hands, axes destroy. In the right hands, they facilitate numerous good outcomes—like frontier settlements.

(I realize that if grandpa were beheading a chicken in the moment you came around the barn it would have reinforced your original distortion. But this is my story, and that never happened.)

This discovery would be counterintuitive. It's weird, but axes are honorable. Decent people own them. People like your grandfather. In some instances, they lead to stew. Your perspective toward axes would be forever altered by this realization. That moment beside the barn would be transformative. Like discovering there's no Santa Claus, but in a good way. The truth about axes—which came to you much too late—would change your outlook. Axes are decent. You might even go so far as to buy an axe and use it—for good.

Obviously this newfound clarity would not be without some difficulty. Inevitably it would battle against your previous experience. After all, it's hard to unthink something as graphic as *Saw I–III*.

Given your initial exposure to axes, disturbing thoughts, images, and emotions would remain imbedded in your memory bank. They would occasionally rise up at the mere sight of an axe. You would struggle in your thought life to keep axes in their proper context. How could it not be a challenge?

> Flee immorality. Every other sin that a man commits is outside the body, but the immoral man sins against his own body. Or do you not know that your body is a temple of the Holy Spirit who is in you, whom you have from God, and that you are not your own? For you have been bought with a price: therefore glorify God in your body (1 Corinthians 6:18-20).

In the end, you wish you'd never seen those previous images. You regret your unsupervised discovery of axes and innocence lost. You do what any reasonable man would do in your situation: You begin teaching your son the truth about axes. No sense in him living with the same deception.

IMAGINE A GOOD MAN

Now imagine a husband. Six feet tall, 215 pounds. Happily married for more than ten years. He and his bride enjoy a healthy and normal physical relationship. He's a faithful husband and father with no major imbalances. A very dependable spouse, dad, and friend with a life you could set your watch by. He obviously loves his family and his Lord. He's extraordinarily normal. You know the kind.

Then one day his wife—attempting to access the Internet on his laptop—inadvertently opens up a file. To her shock she sees images so indecent she instinctually snaps the laptop closed. Horrifying. She gasps. It takes her a moment to figure it out. Initially she assumes there's some mistake. But upon further investigation it all hits home. She had no clue. Her marriage is a statistic.

Anger. Horror. Disappointment. Disgust. Embarrassment. Rejection. Her world comes apart for a few days. Finally, in front of their pastor, she discovers how deep the root goes. It's been going on since before they were married. It goes all the way back to junior high. It's overwhelming. Confused, she asks the one question every wife in this situation asks: "How is it possible to live this lie and say you love me?" While it does not take away the pain, or make sense of the madness of sin, there is an answer—imagine an axe.

More importantly, imagine a young boy whose first exposure to sex was a grotesque misrepresentation. Somewhere in a locker room or the back of a bus an image appeared. An image for which he was not prepared. So powerful it conjured up the type of feelings no boy his age should experience. Feelings intended for a specific place and time in his life. Once the image makes its mark, there's no going back. Like a word you hear constantly after hearing it for the first time, the images are unrelenting. Ads suggest wearing the right body spray will bring a mass of sexual experiences for the "average" male. Images come at him from everywhere. Soon he's seeking them out.

Like assuming axes are exclusive to horror films, he's left to assume that sex is base. Perverted and nasty. The images seem to indicate women enjoy being treated like objects of self-indulgence. So that affects his perception. The overall message? Women are to be conquered and denigrated. Real men view women this way and have as much sex as they can. So that's what he sets out to do. Sex is everything and the most satisfying reality on earth. Everything else pales in comparison.

A JOURNEY INTO DARKNESS

And so his journey into darkness begins. In the light he's a businessman, bus driver, doctor, or deacon. In the shadows of his life, however, lurks a dark and despairing secret. It hounds him mercilessly. He both hates it and loves what it promises. He has sweet seasons of victory over its power and then falls headlong back in with little or no warning. Over and over he's betrayed by his own stupidity.

Then one day he meets a girl and falls in love. This relationship is different from the rest. This girl opens his eyes to the beauty of marriage. Like coming around the back of a barn, he realizes the truth about sex and its design. It's not shameful, intended solely for self-gratification. God created it to be a good thing. It is not something for which he should feel shame. In marriage it's both satisfying and undefiled. It finds its true meaning in this specific context. In this place it can be pure and selfless.

He leaves the previous corruption behind to enjoy the bride of his youth. All is well and as God intended. Then one day, after the novelty of newlyweddedness fades, he encounters an image on a billboard. Unexpectedly, the slow pull of that old force draws him back in. He ignores it one day only to heed it the next. So it goes, until he lingers longer at an image than he should. Eventually there are files on his hard drive. She is a once-naïve, now-broken wife.

Unfortunately, this is not a hypothetical situation. The statistics surrounding porn are unbelievable and not so hard to believe at the same time. The pervasive power of porn never ceases to amaze me. With frightening frequency it's more often reality. More men than I'd like to admit have sobbed like little children in my office confessing their pathetic secret. The web of self-deceit is complex and mind-blowing.

From here the story takes predictable paths. The husband unthinkingly dumps the whole reality into the wife's lap without warning. (Not a good idea.) Henceforth, he tells his wife every time he has any immoral thought. This guts the wife.

Men in this situation have this strange ability to make themselves the victim and garner their wives' sympathy. All the while the real victim, the wife, is buried under an avalanche of the husband's struggle. The intense focus on his battle with porn and penchant for masturbation becomes the marriage's identity. It ends up being all about him, again.

Eventually he joins with a group of men in therapy who sit around and discuss their struggles ad nauseam. They couch their sin in more noble terms like *addiction*. They perpetually misdiagnose the problem and repent of the wrong things. They rely on inadequate steps for prevention—usually technology and strength in numbers—and repeat the cycle of failure, exposure, repentance, restoration, victory, temptation, failure, sin.

NO EASY ANSWER

Innumerable theories exist as to where the struggle comes from. Some well-respected preachers have suggested deep psychological reasons such as profound loneliness, or emptiness brought on by the idolatry of our culture. Others have pointed to low morals and insufficient levels of fear toward God and consequences. Some point to the curse and its gravity-like effects on the male libido. None of this, however, can supply an answer sufficient to account for the epidemic struggle we're facing with porn.

Ultimately, the reason so many Christian men struggle with porn is due to a vacancy in their character. Their person cannot handle the weighty responsibility of sexuality because they're completely unprepared for it. They're still reacting to it as if they were twelve years old. Their unsupervised adolescence comes back to haunt them when they're twenty-five. Inside they're still perverted little boys. I wish it were more complicated than this, but it's not. This is not to suggest that a complexity of issues is not involved, but that the root issue is basic. Lust overwhelms them and they lack the self-control to push it back.

Paul identified it as a lust of "deceitful desires" (Ephesians 4:22 ESV). Which is the best description you'll ever find. That's because deceit is the prime source of its power. Paul did not mean that *we* are lustful deceivers (although we are), but that *lust* is deceitful by nature. Lust is a bald-faced lie. It guarantees us that unbridled hedonism is the ultimate aim of life. It creates and then feeds on the unmet desire of our flesh. This is why most everyone who struggles with porn also has a vein of discontent running through his life. (It's the same reason that apparently happy husbands up and leave their wives when their wives' physical appearance diminishes with age.)

TURNING MEN INTO IDIOTS ONE LIE AT A TIME

Lust promises that physical pleasure can deliver a deep unequaled and sustainable satisfaction. But it always delivers something else—heart-wrenching dissatisfaction. That's because it's a liar. Never delivering what it promises. It results in the exact opposite.

Lust is a master deceiver and porn is its masterpiece. Porn is lust in its most tantalizing form. It leaves nothing to the imagination. As such, porn is the most blatant of all lust's lies. It's a hideous beast that mercilessly pummels its victims. Like lambs to a slaughter it turns otherwise strong, smart, and successful men into idiots. Men who risk careers, reputation, incomes, and family to sneak peeks on company computers that they know have filters and tracking software, or fall headlong into binges of visual excess while on a business trip, charging porn to credit cards they know have records.

It's all a lie. We know it's not real. We know it will never deliver. We know too well how it destroys people and marriages. Yet we believe what it says. Every time we do it mocks us for our stupidity. No wonder the father in Proverbs confronted his son with a similar warning: "On account of a harlot one is reduced to a loaf of bread, and an adulteress hunts for the precious life." Or, to put that colloquially, "Hey, moron! Don't be stupid!"

None of it's true. Just step back and look at the insanity for a moment. That ubiquitous billboard is not true. Those lyrics about the joy of a no-strings-attached sexual escapade are not true. Those women are not in ecstasy. They are in agony. They are the collateral damage of a negligent father. A daughter formerly in pigtails now being used in fiendish ways, never having found male affection in any other context.

Those men are not the happiest people on earth. They're morons to whom no real woman would actually give the time of day. They're lonely shells.

Those people in gratuitous sex scenes in movies who collapse madly in love don't exist. They're actually self-absorbed actors whose own lives are disasters. Shallow narcissists on their fourth or fifth marriage.

Hugh Hefner is an utterly decadent old man who used his position and power within the porn industry to secure sexual conquests. At present, he's at the end of his life. Those people at his parties aren't his friends. Those women around him keeping the king warm in the cold of his twilight could care less. They're only there because of his money and power. The same reason any of them has ever been on his arm. He knows it. The charade is over. He's going to die alone and lonely. And every time we ogle some other man's wife with our eyes or gratify ourself with an image we're just like him. Ridiculous.

RELIEF, REGRET, AND REPENTANCE

Ask any man who struggles with porn and he'll tell you it's the pursuit of the image that most mesmerizes him. Not the consummation of sin. It's not the act of indulgence that lures most, but the anticipation of it. This is all it can offer. A hollow promise. This is why men feel such an emotional collapse of shame when they gratify themselves with pornography. Once the chase is over, the pathetic truth is out.

But if we know all this, then why do so many men idiotically destroy reputation, marriage, and family for a fleeting rush of pleasure? Especially when the result is always the same—a frustrating, nauseating emptiness? Honest answer? Who really knows? Simple answer? We're sinners.

The yarn lust spins is the one lie our sinful nature wishes were true above all others. It touches a deep root of confusion and wickedness in us. We are the center of the universe and our pleasure is supreme. At our core we are idolaters who worship self and all our sins are a symptom of this reality. The struggle with pornography is a symptom and not the root. We do these things not because we are victims of an unseen force working against us, but because we want to do them. Ultimately, however, sin is madness and there's no good explanation.

Of course no one understands the insanity of it all more than the man caught in pornography's gears. It's like a scene out of *A Beautiful Mind*. He—more than anyone else—realizes how ridiculous it is. He would never attempt to offer a rational explanation as to why he keeps hurling himself into porn's teeth. Since no rationale exists. I promise you, no one thinks it more ridiculous than he. A man can begin to think that he's crazy...and alone. Such is the sinister hollowness of this sin. It taunts men like a vindictive master. Defeat. Despair. Hopelessness. The vicious cycle of its tyranny.

No wonder men who are "found out" usually react with a mixture of pain and relief. *Pain* in what they've done, who they've disappointed and those sinned against, especially God Himself. *Relief* comes as the light of truth floods into their darkness. By the time it's all out they're exhausted by the energy they've spent keeping it under wraps. Shame, one of sin's many shackles, keeps them from seeking help. Fearing rejection or more concrete consequences, they live behind a façade of moralism.

You can rail against him and he will agree with you. You can threaten consequences and he will welcome them. You can predict tragedies and he will acknowledge their potential. You are preaching to the choir, my friend. He gets it. He knows it is crazy. "Can you help me out of this?" he begs.

Most often, we don't know how to help. The church—while trying to respond—has struggled to deal with it. As statistics pile up the church labors with how to react. Our fundamentalist conclaves have left us bewildered at the current outbreak of confessions. Many would like to go back to a time when no one talked about these things and people were content to suffer in silence. This, ironically, is one of the very reasons we find ourselves here now. But when a decent, well-respected man whom no one suspects steps forward out of desperation to confess a decades-long struggle, the naïveté of our mind-set is shattered. There is no going back.

Our standard knee-jerk reaction is to throw a rope of moralism down to him and encourage him to pull himself up by it. "Pull yourself up!" we shout from on high. We think we're being helpful. In reality, we are merely assuming the gospel (see chapter 2). Without coming out and saying it, we consider the gospel powerless to help with such sophisticated struggles. This neglect of the gospel makes one wonder who's really crazy: The suffering sinner, or the well-meaning Christian friend who overlooks the one message that provides hope.

For instance, we offer accountability (software, groups, etc.). While helpful, generally useful, and a normal part of church life, it is not a complete solution. If a man is willing to lie to his own conscience, he will lie to people he loves and respects. Wife. Pastor. Family. Friends. Besides, offering the disappointment of others as a motivator for change is an additional type of bondage. If this is the extent of our service, we have laid a burden back on him "not even our fathers could bear." The gospel lifts the burden of self-help off of the victims we have unwittingly placed it on.

It sounds foolish to us (as Paul said it would) and nearly counter-intuitive given our love for self-salvation, but this man needs to be reminded that he is accepted by God through the finished work of Jesus Christ. That he can stop striving to be perfect and start resting in Christ's perfection. God has already forgiven him for his failure to be a perfect human being, an ideal man, and spotless husband. The grace of God will help him repent of the root and not just the symptom.

Our Savior descended the rope down into our despair. He sacrificed Himself for us within view of our idolatry. He wept for its tyranny over us. He died to free us from its bondage. The cross is the remedy. It *unequivocally* refuses any help we might offer to improve our condition before God, which cannot be improved or diminished. He is righteous. Unless "Christ died needlessly" (Galatians 2:21). It *simultaneously* reminds us that our problem is not behavioral or circumstantial, but internal. We need a divine remedy and not a superficial one. "A man is not justified by the works of the Law but through faith in Christ Jesus" (Galatians 2:16). *Ultimately*, the cross teaches us how to live. From it we find the true meaning of love. Here is the power over lust and its hold on us. Sacrificial love and self-sacrifice brought to us in the cross of Christ and free us from the self-indulgent shackles pornography binds to our desires.

OVERCOMING POLYESTER AND PLASTIC DAYDREAMS

When I think of my own sons' future in the cesspool we call society, I cringe. This beast lurks out there. If I love them I'll sound the alarm. To do otherwise would be like handing my sons a snake. What idiot wouldn't talk to his son about the dangers of pornography and the intoxicating power of graphic immorality? (That's rhetorical. Don't answer that.)

We have to take action. In light of the tsunami of immorality that pours into our world every day, we have to. Some strongly urge accountability via Internet firewalls and groups of men. But every man I know who is addicted to porn knows how to get around both. Some recommend therapy with specialists in the field. But every man I know in formal therapy ends up unintentionally doing the very thing he's trying to stop—making his struggle the center of his universe. In many instances we're just managing symptoms. I believe there is something we can do to prepare those headed into this firestorm and treat those who have been consumed by it. Fair warning: If you live in a polyester and plastic daydream of Christian "swirly twirly gumdrops" you need to buckle up! You are not going to like this. It's not going to be easy, but here's what needs to happen.

First, if I want to fortify my sons' lives against this barrage of perversion headed their way and rescue those currently under seige, I have to tell them the truth. Not only about the deception of porn, but also about the incredible alternative. That's right *Mr. Cleaver*. You need to tell that teenage boy (Captain Hormone) in your house the truth about sex. In our many efforts to stem the tide we rarely ever consider this. If God created sex, then there is a sense in which it's decent and pure. The exact opposite version of the world's corruption. It's a new way to look at an axe.

I realize this is exactly opposite of what we normally do and how we've been conditioned to respond. Usually we learn of our son's struggle after it's exposed. We react by ripping computers and TVs out of the wall. We put accountability software on our home computers. We batten down the hatches. We stop all incoming messages. This has little effect on the heart of the young man. To depend solely upon restricting access to images and information is a fundamental misunderstanding of the real problem—the human heart. Point is, you may stop porn from getting onto your son's computer, but you can't stop the reel running in his head. Only the gospel can get in there.

What I want to do is get upstream and start preparing my son's heart with the biblical perspective. You just can't stop the wrong stuff from getting in. You have to allow the right stuff to find its way into his heart and soul. You can't only tell him what to run *from*. You have to tell him what to run *to*. Maybe you're afraid to do that because you think being honest about the biblical view of sex will corrupt him. Hello! He's already corrupted. This is the very reason he can't translate sex properly. Without a biblical grid inserted into his mind, he's lost.

IT IS BETTER THAN CHOCOLATE

So, tell your son the truth. Sex is full-on one of the most amazing experiences he can imagine. And trust me, he will imagine. In fact, you need to tell him it's better than he imagines. It's going to blow his mind. In this sense, you are admitting the grain of truth in the world's deception. But, you're taking it back and putting it in context. Yes, it is pleasurable. But that's only part of the truth.

Physical pleasure, while desirable and not necessarily sinful, is not the most satisfying experience in life. The gospel—the most satisfying reality known to man—makes sex satisfying in ways the world can never know. The instant gratification of unattached sex is not the ultimate aim of life. There are greater realities that make sex make sense and put it in its proper place. Our job is to tell the truth. Either we do that, or he'll succumb to the ruse of immorality.

To put it plainly, I want my sons to so anticipate the joy of sex with their future wives from a Christian perspective so that when the "harlot" lurking on the corner of this culture offers them something different, it seems absurd. Long term, I want to preserve my sons' opportunity (and that of my future daughters-in-law) to experience sex in the purity and freedom for which it was designed. I pray they are so eager about the liberating innocence of a physical relationship with their wives that they never buy into the hollow promise of sexual immorality. I want billboards to seem stupid, not alluring. I want them to pray for Hugh Hefner's empty soul, not envy him. After all, before God they are no better than Hugh and he no more beyond saving than they.

Without crossing the line of decency with our sons, we need to establish as quickly as possible that the biblical perspective of sex far surpasses any of the nonsense out there. We can't pretend sex doesn't exist. We can't suggest it's not satisfying on a certain level. It is. We must tell the truth. In order for this to happen we have to create an environment where we can talk about it honestly and openly. Why wouldn't we? Why can't we communicate to our sons the same thing the Bible does?

> Drink water from your own cistern and fresh water from your own well. Should your springs be dispersed abroad, streams of water in the streets? Let them be yours alone and not for strangers with you. Let your fountain be blessed, and rejoice in the wife of your youth. As a loving hind and a graceful doe, let her breasts satisfy you at all times; be exhilarated always with her love. For why should you, my son, be exhilarated with an adulteress and embrace the bosom of a foreigner? (Proverbs 5:15-20).

THE CHURCH BROUGHT A KNIFE TO A GUNFIGHT

The world dominates the airwaves when it comes to sex and sexuality. Even in the church. Most teens in the church get their view of sex from MTV. The secular media absolutely crushes our message. For that matter, we don't have one. Our default position is silence. Basically, the church has brought a knife to a gunfight.

Obviously we're not competing for the same goals, but this is a battle nonetheless. We hold the truth and shouldn't be afraid to wield it. We should be telling our children the truth—all of it. Sex is exhilarating. Instead, even with our own children, we react in puritanical prudishness. Yes, we're supposed to flee the corrupting influence of the world's sleaze. But if we think filtering images on our Internet service represents a comprehensive approach to guiding our children in sexuality, we're as ignorant as they are.

I don't want my sons to feel shame at the thought of sex. I want them to think of it the right way. I want them to respect it. I want them to esteem it rightly through the lens of a biblical worldview. In a sense,

I want to take away the mystery (which the world uses to lure them) without robbing it of the purity. That is, I want to properly represent it without cheapening it.

Second, I'm going to let my sons off the hook. I'm going to tell them the desire they have on a physical level is natural and not necessarily sinful. They are supposed to want to have sex. It's normal. They are supposed to be attracted to members of the opposite sex. That too is natural. I'm sorry Ward, but there you have it. If I don't tell them, they'll go stark raving mad.

From a physiological point of view it's inevitable. When your son nears twelve, watch his eyes near the cash register at the grocery store. Where does that impulse come from? Same place yours did. You can point his eyes in the right direction if you don't ignore it.

Your job is to guide him through all the changes he experiences as he grows. You have to speak into the awkwardness and confusion. You have to make sure he does not cover what is a normal experience for a young man with a fig leaf of shame. You don't want him hiding in darkness from all this stuff. You want him to face it in light of the truth.

Third, and most important, I'm going to saturate my sons' lives with the gospel and the cross of Jesus Christ. Even if I cut off access to the Internet, only the gospel can purify the reel running in his head. Sex as the world sells it is utterly selfish. As is obvious, the world is phenomenal at moving the product. Fundamentally, it's about instant gratification at the expense of some other human being. People are objects for pleasure and self is supreme. It's characterized by the unbridled pursuit of personal pleasure. The cross is the only effective filter for this nonsense.

BARN DOORS AND ROAMING COWS

By the time a son has accessed porn it's way too late. Honestly, what rock have his parents been living under? When it's finally discovered they frantically start taking action. Which is like slamming the barn door after the cows are out. Parents show up in my office asking for help. "I've neglected my responsibilities with him for the past eighteen years. Can you help? I've got an hour over lunch...not taking the drive time into consideration, of course."

The opposite of hedonistic excess is selfless sacrifice. That's the message of the cross. This is the place sex makes sense. If I want my sons to disdain the basic message of porn I have to expose them to the glory of sacrificial love as observed in the cross of Jesus Christ. True joy and fulfillment is found in service to others, not using others.

As the world would have you believe, sexual gratification is the greatest experience known to man. If that were how God intended it, then there would be sex between husband and wife in heaven. But Jesus made it clear that won't happen (Luke 20:34-36).

Do you love your son? Talk to him. Tell him the truth about sex—and the sacrificial love of the gospel.

> At the window of my house I looked out through my lattice, and I saw among the naïve, I discerned among the youths a young man lacking sense, passing through the street near her corner; and he takes the way to her house, in the twilight, in the evening, in the middle of the night and in the darkness (Proverbs 7:6-9).

14

ETERNITY:
LIVE URGENTLY

*This I say, brethren, the time has been shortened, so that from now
on those who have wives should be as though they had none; and
those who weep, as though they did not weep; and those who rejoice,
as though they did not rejoice; and those who buy, as though they
did not possess; and those who use the world, as though they did not
make full use of it; for the form of this world is passing away.*

{ 1 CORINTHIANS 7:29-31 }

A middle-aged woman can amass an impressive list of excuses as to why she should not participate in a short-term mission trip. Leaving her husband and children for so long does not seem right. Who would do all the stuff while she was gone? The kids like the crust cut off their bread just so. Besides, a person does not have to go overseas to participate in missions anyway. Missions is across the street as much as it is across the pond. Besides, she was a middle-aged wife and mother. She had nothing to contribute. She was no sort of specialist. What if she were captured by savage natives? She'd seen pictures of fierce-looking men in loincloths with bones in their noses. (Of course she saw bone-wearing teenagers down at the mall, but they seemed harmless.) But if she were captured, who would do the laundry? She might also contract a mysterious illness. She'd heard the horror stories about parasites. She could die. She may never come home. She might get diarrhea. It was all too intimidating. The thought of going was about as far out of her comfort zone as she could get. She never went.

Then one day near her fiftieth birthday this middle-aged woman surprised everyone, especially herself. She signed up to go. She had passed the registration table in the church lobby one too many times. It was like playing with fire. Eventually, it got her. She was finally venturing out of her predictable world and going on a short-term trip with her local church. She wasn't just going "around the corner." She was headed to the Congo. Of all the destinations she could have chosen for her first trip, she was bound for one of the remotest and most dangerous places on the planet. Diarrhea here we come!

Needless to say, she was anxious. Excited, but uneasy. The preparations were a lot of work. She paced through the normal litany of procedures and processes required for departure. Fundraising. She had to mail letters convincing friends and family of the importance of this trip. Planning. The group would be involved in a myriad of projects once they arrived. Of course, all these projects could end up changing before they landed and all their careful planning would be moot. They might actually have to live by faith. Meetings. Throughout the process there were dozens of meetings after church. She was dubbed the strategic administrator prior to departure. Turns out moms can organize a thing or two.

Team-building. The team had a few get-togethers to foster camaraderie. Each participant shared the stories of God's grace in their lives. The fervor for sharing the gospel was reignited as she eavesdropped on its power in others' lives. Presentations. She had to stand in front of the church on a Sunday morning. Her husband was all smiles. Medical. She subjected herself to a battery of painful shots. Apparently they would help ward off all the diseases she could barely pronounce. Her blood could set off a Geiger counter by the time they left. Departure. She prepared for the worst, but was thrilled about the opportunity. It was a once-in-a-lifetime deal. She hated good-byes at airports.

THREE LITTLE LETTERS

At some point in the run-up to departure she sat down and wrote three letters. One for each of her three daughters. It was a rather dramatic moment. If for some reason she did not return home, she wanted a record of "everything" she would want to say to them. So she sat down and spelled it all out. Everything. I love you. Love the Lord. Here's how to be a godly wife. Be good mothers. I'm proud of you. She filled three letters with a mother's love and wisdom. She sealed them. Got on a plane and headed for parts unknown.

Of course, she did come home. She had survived the dangers of the Congo for the sake of the gospel. The trip changed her life. It was amazing, to say the least. She had a new perspective on life. For a few moments she lived life like God intended it to be lived every day. She should have gone sooner.

The experience was life-transforming. She was pressed way beyond the ordinary. She saw God work in and through the team. Distinct moments indelibly marked her. The Bible studies with the group on the floor of the jungle. Somehow way out there in nothingness the Word of God fashioned new ears for her. It meant more than it had ever meant. It was rich. The team members. She learned the power of common servants. The missionaries. They were ordinary people— businessmen and moms—sent to do extraordinary work in the name of Christ. She came back with a part of her left behind and the rest of her filled up with meaning.

OUR BRIEF ENCOUNTERS WITH LIFE

If you've ever been on a short-term mission trip, you know what a remarkable experience it is. All of it. It tests and blesses a person's soul like few things can. You step out of the rat race for a moment and into an experience unfamiliar to the rest of your life. For a few brief weeks you live as you were meant to live. You live urgently.

There is an enormous buildup of excitement and clarity. You write letters. There is a focus of life and contemplation that happens in few other contexts. The truly important realities in life become, well, important. You love people. As the grist of the routine is washed off by the new, you begin to take notice of others around you. You live not from paycheck to paycheck, but friendship to friendship. On buses and planes and in huts your days are filled with meaningful conversations.

These never happen stateside. There's no cell phone coverage in the middle of nowhere to interrupt you. You are passionate. You live for the glory of God and the name of Jesus Christ in a concentrated moment. There is a feverish digging down into significant things of eternity. Time seems more precious. With clearly stated objectives and time frames pressed up against return trips, no moment is wasted.

Each evening you gather with the team to recalibrate and refocus so as not to squander the remaining moments. What are we here for? is the question at every meeting. Resources are invaluable. The money it takes to buy groceries for one week back home can feed a village for a month in other places. Every dime is dispensed for maximum impact. Pennies make such a difference. For once, mammon serves you. You haven't been to Starbucks in weeks. That's $500 extra right there. Energy is exhausted. You push yourself way out of your comfort zone. Your back hurts. It's a strangely fulfilling pain. Minds are focused like laser beams. Hearts are filled. Christ has never been so real. Love is abundant. You miss your family. Those oft-neglected relationships are now inestimable (Philippians 1:6-8). The gospel is everything (Romans 1:16).

These trips change us, but for a moment only. There is peculiar backfire to them. They are extraordinary windows in our experience that make normal life anything but surprising. They create a contrast between missions and everyday life that is an unfortunate side effect. The intense focus doesn't last. We come home and get right back to being what we were before. Same routines. Same jobs. Same activities. We stop by Starbucks on our way to church and don't drop anything in the offering plate once we get there. It's a weird form of dementia. We forget to ask the question, "Why are we here?" We should go on more short-term trips.

When we forget to ask, we never truly live. But here's the thing: life itself is a short-term mission trip for the redeemed. All the same dramatic features are present all around. Life on this earth is short. "Therefore be careful how you walk, not as unwise men but as wise, making the most of your time, because the days are evil" (Ephesians 5:15-16).

We're strangers in a foreign land.

> Peter, an apostle of Jesus Christ, to those who reside as aliens, scattered throughout Pontus, Galatia, Cappadocia, Asia, and Bithynia, who are chosen according to the foreknowledge of God the Father, by the sanctifying work of the Spirit, to obey Jesus Christ and be sprinkled with His blood: May grace and peace be yours in fullest measure (1 Peter 1:1-2).

We're on a mission field.

> Jesus came up and spoke to them, saying, "All authority has been given to Me in heaven and on earth. Go therefore and make disciples of all the nations, baptizing them in the name of the Father and the Son and the Holy Spirit, teaching them to observe all that I commanded you; and lo, I am with you always, even to the end of the age" (Matthew 28:18-20).

We have a message to proclaim.

> You are a chosen race, a royal priesthood, a holy nation, a people for God's own possession, that you may proclaim the excellencies of Him who has called you out of darkness into His marvelous light (1 Peter 2:9).

We have work to do.

> We proclaim Him, admonishing every man and teaching every man with all wisdom, so that we may present every man complete in Christ. For this purpose also I labor, striving according to His power, which mightily works within me (Colossians 1:28-29).

We're always headed home.

> Blessed be the God and Father of our Lord Jesus Christ, who according to His great mercy has caused us to be born again to a living hope through the resurrection of Jesus Christ from the dead, to obtain an inheritance which is

imperishable and undefiled and will not fade away, reserved in heaven for you, who are protected by the power of God through faith for a salvation ready to be revealed in the last time (1 Peter 1:3-5).

We should view ourselves as missionaries simply because we are. When you live so you live differently, you *are* a missionary. Your church is your sending agency. Your home is your headquarters. Your car is your transport vehicle. Your money is your support. Your family is your team. Your job is your cover. Your neighbors are your immediate field. Your life is the gospel. Life is a short-term mission trip. You have been sent by God. Where you live is your "end of the earth." Live it.

THE DANGEROUS LIVES OF LIBERATED PEOPLE

It's not that we look forward to escaping this place. We're not escapists. We are acutely engaged in the here and now as few others can be. We see right through the temporariness the world so highly prizes. Those same things we once prized. We live urgently now. We look around us to the unsaved and share the love of God in Christ as we move forward and look to greater realities. We point past the temporal. It's our intention to drag as many pagans with us into eternity as we can. We're not detached vagabonds. We're uniquely stationed emissaries of the risen Savior and returning Judge. We have been set free from the here and now, but desire to bless it with eternity. We are dangerous people on this planet. Dangerous I say. You have to believe this to truly live. It changes everything.

Possessions. Whereas all our decisions were once shaped by materialism, they are now shaped by unseen realities. The conviction that the most important things in life are those we can touch and accumulate is gone. This is not all there is. Accumulating more and holding on to what we have are not the ambitions of our heart any longer. "For where your treasure is, there your heart will be also" (Matthew 6:21).

Pleasure. We used to live as hedonists. Our obsession in life was the empty satisfaction of immediate gratification. No longer. "Lay aside the old self, which is being corrupted in accordance with the lusts of deceit" (Ephesians 4:22).

Anger. We no longer waste life's opportunities in the sour resentment of disadvantages or hurts. We live life with an edge of contentment and not bitterness. We live in light of the infinite debt forgiven in Jesus Christ. "Be angry, and yet do not sin; do not let the sun go down on your anger" (Ephesians 4:26).

Fear. We were inhibited by the insecurity of what we could not control or didn't know. In the view of eternity we can finally let go and trust in the perfect ways of God. "Even though I walk through the valley of the shadow of death, I fear no evil; for You are with me; Your rod and Your staff, they comfort me" (Psalm 23:4).

Success. We were once driven by the perception of our peers. Status and achievement were what got us out of bed in the morning. From the cradle to the grave we were taught that finding wealth and success brought happiness. Now our happiness is untouchable. "Whoever wishes to save his life will lose it; but whoever loses his life for My sake will find it" (Matthew 16:21).

Leisure. Our gods were once security and comfort. Hobbies, activities, and sports sapped all our energy. Now our moments are filled with people—our wives, children, and friends.

Regret. Who we were has found its match in the righteousness of Jesus Christ. We have been set free.

> It is a trustworthy statement, deserving full acceptance, that Christ Jesus came into the world to save sinners, among whom I am foremost of all. Yet for this reason I found mercy, so that in me as the foremost, Jesus Christ might demonstrate His perfect patience as an example for those who would believe in Him for eternal life (1 Timothy 1:15-16).

Envy. We once lived discontented lives as we obsessed about our station in life, our possessions or personal abilities. There was deep dissatisfaction. Now our discontent is holy. God, for whom we hunger and thirst, is infinite and beyond comprehension. "Whom have I in heaven but You? And besides You, I desire nothing on earth. My flesh and my heart may fail, but God is the strength of my heart and my portion forever" (Psalm 73:25-26).

One morning, not long after this middle-aged woman's return from the Congo, as was the routine, she was awakened by her cat. She got up briefly to open the curtains, then lay back down. When she got back down in her bed, she died instantly of a massive heart attack. Barely a sound, and she was gone. Needless to say, this was a shock. She had just celebrated her fiftieth birthday. Truth is, one's bedroom is no less dangerous than the Congo. We just never know. There is an ever-present urgency.

Later her daughters had the difficult task of sorting through their mother's possessions. They came across three letters. There, written in her own hand, was everything their mother wanted to say to them should she not live to see another day. The discovery was a treasure beyond value. Their mother had left little undone. For that brief moment when she lived fully, she saw clearly enough not to take anything for granted.

15

CONSISTENCY: LEARN TO PLOD

*There is nothing better for a man than to eat and drink and tell himself
that his labor is good. This also I have seen that it is from the hand of God.*

{ ECCLESIASTES 2:24 }

Mike was a high school football hero. I remember standing in awe of him on game days at our school as he and his comrades made the "spirit walk" around campus on the way to the pep rally. I'd run beside him along the route. There's nothing quite as cool to a lowerclassman as an upperclassman donning his jersey on a school day. Well, that and the cheerleaders. It was this spectacle on Fridays during the season that first drew my heart into sports. Ahhh. Football in the South. These guys were larger than life. But elementary-age boys know very little of the real world.

One Saturday night Mike was out with a fellow football player. Their VW bug crossed paths with a pulpwood truck on a narrow country road in the dark of night. Mike was the passenger. The driver, who was also a football player, survived with a few broken bones. A few nights later he was in his own bed. Mike, on the other hand, clung to life. He had sustained a severe head injury and lay in a coma for weeks.

I remember visiting the ICU waiting room while a vigil over his life was taking place. Heartrending anxiety filled the air. Miraculously, Mike pulled through and awoke from his coma. But he was never the same. He had suffered severe brain damage. Nonetheless, there was much rejoicing. His parents would take a broken-down son over the alternative. I remember Mike's dad raising his hands to heaven in the hospital, tearfully thanking God for saving his son.

There were no more spirit walks for Mike. In fact, walking was a challenge. He had little use of his right side. His arm, which he held close to his body, was permanently bent at the elbow. He dragged his right foot laboring to walk. A mere shadow of the athletic young man he was before the accident.

Despite his ordeal, Mike wasn't angry. I remember very vividly the image and sound of Mike shuffling down the halls of our school. Mike's mouth bent upward in a permanent smile. He did not want sympathy. He had been humbled by the whole ordeal. He was happy to be alive. Rather than existing in bitterness, he accepted his life with peace. He eventually entered into the ministry. More than one person was inspired by Mike. A different type of heroism was undertaken—life.

MORE THAN TREES FELL

Not too long after Mike's wreck, at around age fourteen, I turned into the biggest punk within a five-mile radius of any place I was standing. I was beginning to rebel against authority. My father, aware he had begun to lose my ear, took action.

One morning in the early summer he drove me several miles into the farmland near our home. We pulled into a pasture belonging to Mike's family. There in the distance were several trees Mike's dad had felled the day before. They were cut into two-foot segments along their lengths. Upon seeing their lengths, I knew my fate was not good.

I don't know if Mike's dad had requested my services, or if my father had requested his. Me a surrogate son, or him a surrogate father. Looking back now I would guess the real aim was not so much cutting lumber as it was cutting me down to size. Regardless, it was effective.

The two dads exchanged words and handshakes. Mine drove off. Armed with a thermos of water, sack lunches, gloves, and axes we started at one end of a tree. Mike's dad was a machine. The old man never seemed to tire. I, on the other hand, unfamiliar with farm life, would lose balance after a few swings of the axe due to fatigue. My back ached a mere half-hour into the job. I had met my match—hard work.

For those three days Mike was seated on a stump watching me swing away—with a mysterious grin on his face. Given the log truck that put him on that stump, I found it ironic that his dad and I were splitting lumber together. As if we were getting even one tree at a time. I'm not sure anyone except me thought it ironic.

We'd break for lunch each day around noon, sit in the shade, and talk. I mainly listened. They spoke highly of my father, Dr. Yawn, who had been at Mike's bedside through the duration of their suffering. Not surprisingly, there were more than trees that fell on that farm. The sincerity of their relationship hacked away at my obstinate attitude toward my own father. I began to see him in a different light. In the shadow of this father and son I recovered my respect for my own dad.

Unlikely Lumberjacks

In those moments I began to realize how much I took for granted. I knew Mike would have given anything to switch places with me and work alongside his father. Other petty preoccupations of my teenage world began to fade in importance.

I was happy to be a part of this unlikely band of lumberjacks. I was strangely thankful for the blisters and physical ability to work hard. In sight of Mike I saw work for the privilege it is. It does something to the soul of a man to know he has completed a task that takes effort. To step back and see that you've accomplished something by the sweat of your brow is profoundly enriching.

When we began, those trees looked miles long. I thought we'd never finish. But we did. It took three days to cut and stack all the wood. It probably would have taken less without me, but sometimes letting someone learn to do something right is more important than doing it fast. I distinctly remember the satisfaction I felt at the end of the three days. Funny that those humble stacks of wood meant so much to me. Finishing well was the most fulfilling thing I'd ever done.

There's great value in plodding—in doing the same thing persistently with an unswerving commitment to excellence no matter the difficulty, tediousness, or time necessary to do it. As far as desirable qualities goes, plodding isn't as sexy as power or influence, but it's more powerful and influential than either one. It's at the core of many fulfilled lives and time-tested careers.

Those known for finishing usually possess plodding as a trait. Deliberate. Dependable. They finish what they put their hands to because they see the importance of finishing. They look at the length of a tree and see a cord of wood. They look at a career selling copiers and see supporting innumerable industries that make the world go round—including the lumber industry.

William Carey, the father of modern missions, was once asked what secret capacity led to his success. His answer? "I plod." He did the same thing every day with the same enthusiasm as he did the day before. His impact is immeasurable.

To plod is to take a long view of life. Good things take time. They don't come easily. I was rebuked once for discarding a penny I had dropped. The person scooped it up, placed it in his own pocket. Looking at me he said, "That's what dollars are made of." Big things are made of small ones. Lives, careers, and success are built on tiny little details we take the time to pay attention to.

WHAT PENNIES ARE TO DOLLARS

Plodding is to character what pennies are to dollars. Endurance is what character is made of. Self-discipline is the ingredient that forces character to develop. It takes discipline to finish difficult things.

A desire to bypass the time and effort to do something right—most often referred to as laziness—usually signals a deficiency in one's character. These people lack the ability to finish anything because they lack the character that makes the finishing possible. More importantly, those who lack the will to do the hard things are afraid of the pain involved in facing their neglected character. They have never worked hard at anything, so when the time comes to work hard for the thing they want most, they can't.

As an employer, I hire men who have a habit of finishing. What-ever it might be. It's really not the size or significance of the accom-plishment as much as the trend. They must be men driven by principle. This way I can be assured that when the novelty of their job wears off, or they experience a season of hardship, they're not going to bolt. They will see things through.

Men who have a string of start-stops on their resumes will point to various reasons as to why they've resigned those positions. In reality they quit because they know they don't have the chutzpah to last and can't see the value in sticking it out. They see trees and think of blisters. They see copiers and see stereotypes. They move on to repeat the same cycle somewhere else. The real value is in staying put.

ABRAHAM LINCOLN'S
LETTER TO HIS SON'S TEACHER

He will have to learn, I know,
that all men are not just,
all men are not true.
But teach him also that
for every scoundrel there is a hero;
that for every selfish Politician,
there is a dedicated leader...
Teach him for every enemy there is a
friend,

Steer him away from envy,
if you can,
teach him the secret of
quiet laughter.

Let him learn early that
the bullies are the easiest to lick...Teach him, if you can,
the wonder of books...
But also give him quiet time
to ponder the eternal mystery of birds in the sky,
bees in the sun,
and the flowers on a green hillside.

In the school teach him
it is far more honourable to fail
than to cheat...
Teach him to have faith
in his own ideas,
even if everyone tells him
they are wrong...
Teach him to be gentle
with gentle people,
and tough with the tough.

Try to give my son
the strength not to follow the crowd
when everyone is getting on the band wagon...
Teach him to listen to all men...
but teach him also to filter
all he hears on a screen of truth,
and take only the good
that comes through.

Teach him if you can,
how to laugh when he is sad...
Teach him there is no shame in tears,
Teach him to scoff at cynics
and to beware of too much sweetness...
Teach him to sell his brawn
and brain to the highest bidders
but never to put a price-tag
on his heart and soul.

16

THINKING: IF YOU LOWER THE STANDARDS, YOU CAN REACH THEM EVERY TIME

How long, O naïve ones, will you love being simple-minded? And scoffers delight themselves in scoffing and fools hate knowledge?
{ PROVERBS 1:22 }

Life is tough, but it's tougher if you're stupid.
{ JOHN WAYNE IN *THE SANDS OF IWO JIMA* }

F requently, wives have to drag their husbands kicking and screaming to church. It's rare that a husband—inspired by spiritual crisis—decides that church will be a priority for the family. Usually it's the wife who does this. Somewhere along the way she is struck by the seriousness of parenting, sobered by a sudden trial, encouraged by a loving friend's example, or frustrated by the lump of a husband taking root in the couch, and decides to take matters into her own hands.

Mind you, they haven't been to church in five years. This will be tricky. The stratagem (that means "plan") unfolds over dinner something like this. The wife waits until the first bite goes in her husband's mouth (his favorite dish, no doubt) and then sets the hook: "You know, dear, I was thinking...I'd like to visit that church down the street. I hear it's a friendly place. My friend Jan goes there. They have an excellent program for children. The kids could really be encouraged by it. Would you mind if we tried it this Sunday?"

What she really means is "I'm spiritually unfulfilled, lonely, in an ankle-deep existence having been dredged by three children and the consequent episodes of *The Backyardigans.*"

The husband, looking up from his plate, which is festooned (that means "decorated") by elbows at the nine and three o'clock positions, is caught off guard. The look on his face is somewhere between horror and humor. It mocks her. "What? Sure. Whatever. Do they have an early service? Game's on at noon. I don't have to wear a tie, do I?" What he means is "What now? Surely this will pass." It doesn't pass.

LIP-SYNCHING TO THE CLASSICS

They're easy to spot on the following Sunday. She's a bright smile shaking hands with strangers on the way to their seats. "Look at all the adults!" The free childcare makes her weepy.

He's two arms folded, completely out of his element. He cracks me up when he "sings." Consistently the worst lip-synching you'll ever witness. During the sermon he avoids eye contact with the preacher like he's an eight-year-old being lectured by a parent. The pastor sounds condescending (that means "talking down to someone").

When it's all over, he realizes that sitting so deep in the aisle was a tactical error (that means "stratagem"). He'll have to talk with more strangers on the way out. This delay puts the pregame show with the cool hologram-like graphics in jeopardy.

She is thrilled. The Bible was explained and applied. She did not understand it all, but knows she needs to. People were sincere. It's hard to know for sure, but she thinks she saw grown men worshiping alongside their wives and families. For the first time she identifies what's been missing—God.

On the ride home, the not-so-subtle conversation between mom and the kids is the finishing touch. "Mom, it was awesome. They let me use scissors. And did you know there aren't really talking cucumbers in the Bible? Can we go back?" Contented children.

After lunch, she sits by him on the couch and asks, "So what did you think, Honey? It wasn't that bad, was it?" The husband knows he's been bested. He replies, "It was fine, but the preacher used big words. I did not understand half of what he was talking about." This, of course, is redundant (that means "did not need to be said"). It's hard to know for sure, but he thinks he saw grown men crying.

JESUS VS. FOOTBALL

The church has to drag men kicking and screaming out of their leth-argy. Men sit bored in church for years avoiding the vortex of the gos-pel's "edge of your seat" drama. It's impossible for most men to imagine Jesus being more exciting than football. They assume spirituality is a female thing. They also assume big words such as *justification* serve the same purpose as those ubiquitous flower arrangements resting at the foot of the pulpit—for show.

It's not uncommon for men to bail on the church when faced with its implicitly high expectations. Having not read anything greater than the trade journal in their bathroom, the idea of thinking deeply and technically about God threatens to breach the wall of meticulously constructed mediocrity. Pride keeps them from attending Bible stud-ies or men's groups. The mere thought of being asked a direct question about the Bible or to "share" something personal is petrifying.

To be fair, the church hasn't done much to reach men. In fact, it's done just about everything it can to make sure they're never interested. All the dusty mechanics of traditional church make no more sense to him now than they did when he was eight. The only notable difference? The flannel boards have been replaced by Powerpoint. It's the same old monotone message still aimed right over his head (but in flash anima-tion). The point of it all is still lost on him.

THE DANGER OF LOW-LYING FRUIT

Many have realized the error and adjusted the message downward. But even the low-lying fruit of "relevant" preaching and books being offered in bulk haven't really elevated men. They've had the opposite effect. Note to churches and publishers: If you lower the standards, men will reach them every time.

More than one author has documented the effect of the church growth and seeker movements on the male churchgoer. Basically, it's neutered them. It's removed the concept of masculinity from spiritual-ity. According to some, the modern church is geared to reach the emo-tional and spiritual needs of women. In order for men to benefit they must take on a more effeminate spirituality. Ask most men why they attend their current church and the answer is predictable. "My wife likes the worship and they have a great program for kids." The basic message? This church makes my wife happy.

HAVE YOU SEEN *PATTON*?

The men behind the pulpit don't help matters much. Rarely is the preacher the type of guy to whom the man in the pew can relate. Either he's so sanitized they assume he sleeps in a tie, or he's so spiritually androgynous they wonder if he's ever seen *Patton*. Case in point: One of the more popular author/preachers in evangelicalism mentioned on a book dust jacket that his favorite hobby was eating ice cream sundaes. Can you hear the footfall of men running from the pews?

Where is the pastor to whom the average guy can relate? The pastor who spends the bulk of his time descending from "on high" to walk with them through the challenges of being a male in this perverse culture. The one who encourages them upward without pressing them into unrealistic molds. The one who makes the standards appear desirable and achievable without lowering them.

When they get close to him his words and life have a more obvious union, not less. The closer they get, the more similarities they see. At the very same time, the more the difference stands out—an all-encompassing, grace-empowered, fully abandoned pursuit of Christ. His wife, family, children, finances, and hobbies are all filtered through the reality of Christ and His gospel. His aim in life is to have other men do the same. And when you get near him, you do.

If pastors want to move men, they can't insult their intelligence with platitudes, subtle hints, or over-principlized "sermonettes." They must put their proverbial finger in men's faces and tell them exactly why their wife wants to strangle them, or why they're feeling unfulfilled in their careers, or how they've wasted years of spiritual opportunity. Not in belittling harshness, but with frustrated optimism.

The pastor's goal with his men is to refuse the stereotype. Men will always respect the pastor who doesn't mince words, isn't afraid to use big ones, and hands out dictionaries as he pulls them upward to higher ground. Maybe the reason more churches don't offer this type of direct challenge to men is because we too have accepted the culture's stereotype—men are unthinking and dense. We can't expect much out of them so we don't ask.

But this is a mistake. I've been there countless times when men have responded to the challenge and beat the odds. Surprisingly, in no single instance has it occurred because someone made it easy for them. (Ultimately, it happens because of God's grace.) It happens because someone wouldn't take the pressure off and would not accept their excuses. Someone encouraged them to overcome the odds. A friend reached out to them. Someone had the gall to make them think. They placed Calvin, Edwards, Ryle, Warfield, and a dozen other dead thinkers in their hands. Their brain sputtered as they tried to grasp it all, but they repented of pride, admitted their ignorance, and pushed through to clarity.

RASKOLNIKOV AND THE ABILITY TO THINK

Many years ago when I was just beginning to wake my brain from its slumber a friend encouraged me to read Dostoyevsky's *Crime and Punishment*. He didn't hand it to me and say "Read this." It was more subtle. At dinner one night, along with our wives, I listened to him describe its contours and complexity of rich themes. He unintentionally dangled his capacity for contemplation and reflection in front of me and drew me into a weird kind of envy. I actually wanted to think. The joy he had derived from engaging a multifaceted subject on such a deep level was unfamiliar to me.

He described the book as the greatest suspense thriller of all time. Without giving away the end, he shared the basic plot and background. I was hooked. I purchased it. It was then I discovered the masterpiece is over 800 pages long. Needless to say, suspense didn't seem to be its main attribute. It took days of reading just to get Raskolnikov's name right. But I persevered. My friend was so right. As I reached the end, I was on the edge of my seat. The read stretched me beyond my limits. It forced me to look past the obvious into the more substantial themes lying behind the literary genius. Or, it made me think. Pushing my mind like that was an invaluable exercise.

As I listened to my friend that evening, I learned more about myself than I did Russian literature. I was shallow. I was living up to the low standards set on men by the culture. Such a tragic place for a Christian man to find himself. So much depends upon the quality of a man's love of God. So much of his love of God begins with his mind.

When I first came to Christ, a very faithful man—by God's grace—took an interest in me. He was my first pastor. With hundreds of others to care for, he included me in his duties. He knew the importance of men to the church. I remember our very first meeting like it was yesterday. It was in his office. We prayed and then, with little or no explanation, as if time were of the essence, he reached behind him and pulled a paperback New Testament from his shelf. He handed it to me and said, "Okay. There's an Old Testament and there's a New Testament." That was the beginning of the rest of my story. I still own that Bible.

Incredible stuff results from men who are captured by Christ. Men who begin pursuing Him with heart, soul, and mind. It causes a shock wave of inexplicable changes and blessings. A man wins back his wife's confidence, finally leads his kids, conquers his cul-de-sac, reaches his workmates, elevates the church, inspires friends, encourages his pastor, and even gains the respect of his mother-in-law. Well, maybe not his mother-in-law, but it's awesome nonetheless. Lifelong trends are reversed and head off in the right direction.

As the saying goes, it's not *if* you lead, but *where* you lead. The leadership of husbands and fathers is a natural law of the soul. God has designed it this way. If the husband and father loves canoeing, the family goes toward canoeing. If the father likes camping, the family follows suit. It's the way things are. If the husband decides there are more important things than God and family, so does everyone else. If the husband's heart is turned to God, the family will follow. On this level, leadership is not as complicated as we make it. It's what we love demonstrated towards those we love.

When Ordinary Men Catch Fire

If you've ever seen an "ordinary" man catch fire for Christ, you know what I mean. A brush with life does amazing things. Somewhere in some sermon one of those five-dollar words hits home. He begins to think in very personal and very particular ways about God. "Christ died for *me*." "*I* am a sinner." "God had mercy on *me*." "*I* love Christ." "Christ is *my* Lord." The theological phrases and axioms at which he once turned up his nose now define him. Hobbies become hobbies. Priorities become priorities.

One evening this guy darkens the door of the men's Bible study at church. There is a brief moment of stunned silence interrupted by an extended hand and a friendly face. No longer snubbed by his own pride, he sits down and begins the journey deep into the contours of an infinitely more ingenious reality than *The Brothers Karamazov*— the gospel. Like one of those disciples on the road to Emmaus, he has his mind blown by the story of redemption. So much wasted time. He climbs out from under the rock of excuses and gets right to it. The sight of him on Sunday encourages his pastor. His eyes are closed. His face and heart are turned toward heaven. He sings off key, but means every word. It makes the pastor pray for his men.

Let's imagine a different scene at the dinner table. One night, a once-prideful man cries over his plate. His children are startled. It's an unprecedented sight. His wife, who's been praying for months, "gets it" and cries right along with him. She reaches for his hand. Gathering himself, he speaks in humble tones, "I'm sorry I haven't been the husband and father I should be. You are precious treasures to me. God has changed me. I can't really explain it. It's like my eyes have been opened. Christ is so real to me. I love you. I thought we might visit that church down the street. I hear they have a great children's program." And he drags his family skipping and singing to church.

New
International
Version

New Testament

17

WORK:
IT'S A MEANS AND NOT AN END

What does it profit a man to gain the whole world, and forfeit
his soul? For what will a man give in exchange for his soul?
{ MARK 8:36-37 }

T here are specific moments with every man when he looks around at his life and observes who he's become, or begins to wonder at what could have been. It's a box of pictures formerly hidden by clutter pulled from a closet. An hour passes. Tears are shed. It's okay. You're not crazy. I won't tell. It's normal to reflect upon the significance of one's life. Especially those that span decades. Things accumulate—family, kids, careers, etc. Time flies. Babies grow up. It's healthy to think deeply about who you are and what you've accomplished. We should do it more often. A survey at the midway point of a legacy can reveal much about a man. Good and bad.

WE'RE ALL DOOMED! HOW'S MY HAIR?

In more intense forms this type of introspection goes by its more popular name—a mid-life crisis. A man approaches the hazy midpoint of his life and is struck by the speed of time. He starts counting his remaining years on his fingers and panics. Some buy Harleys. Some get hair implants. Some make life- and family-altering mistakes. The shock can be overwhelming. There's no rewind button. There's no going back. "We're all doomed!" Take it from me—it passes. Get back to life. Besides, the minivan is more logical.

There are some men, however, whose entire life is a mid-life crisis. Such a man is caught in the constant cycle of reinventing and restarting. There's a search for purpose that takes him through several iterations of himself. It's the assumption that a different situation, position, or endeavor will bring the life he desires. Stops and starts. The vestiges of "great ideas" are all around. You get the distinct feeling he dislikes himself as much as he envies others. It's a secret regret. His wife—who serves him as a life coach—doesn't understand it, but she lends her support. She loves her husband no matter what he does. But this does not seem to help matters. He spends his entire life living up to some mysterious standard set on him somewhere in the past. The discontent is palpable. You hurt for him.

His work and career serve only to remind him of time wasted, missed opportunities, and the inability to be something he's not. It's a ceiling on life. He's certainly not where he saw himself being. Obviously, we all have seasons when we struggle with the tedium of jobs. Even those who enjoy what they do. But his issue is different. There's a naïve assumption that being who he wished he were, or having the dream job, would solve the restlessness in his soul. Even when he does get the change of employment or promotion he eventually falls back into discontent. His enthusiasm fades. Someone needs to tell him the real problem was not in a box of pictures.

I Need to Get This

Then there's the exact opposite creature. He's defined by his career. He doesn't languish in what he does. He thrives in it. He's good at it. You've seen him. As you stand in front of him, he has his left index finger on his Bluetooth earpiece and his other hand (palm out) in your face as he closes the next deal. He mouths, "Just one second. I need to get this." He is a career. You see him in church and say to yourself, "There's that salesman." Not "There's Jim." Or "There's Bob." What lies in his wake is not missed opportunity (like the first fella), but his family. He's got everything the first man thinks he needs, but at a steep price.

His wife and he come to see me. Sitting in front of me during counseling, their back-and-forth may be the most frequent conundrum upper middle-class couples find themselves in. They went and got their priorities caught in success. She says, "I only want him to be home more often. When he's home I want him to leave work at work." Her confident estimation of the real problem comes with a smug look. She adjusts her tennis bracelet in anticipation of his answer. "I do what I do so you can have the life you have." He rolls his eyes upward, then looks at me. "There's no winning. You see what I have to live with?" I never answer that question. Abruptly, his finger rises to his earpiece. "Sorry. Hold on. I need to get this." She rolls her eyes back. I hurt for them. I think fondly of my wife and kids.

Too many men are identified by their careers, or lack thereof. Some flail about looking for one that will give them meaning. It won't. Others, over time, become better salesmen than they are fathers or husbands. They know their clients more intimately than they know their wife and kids. In each case, there's an imbalance.

FORGETTING WHAT WE'RE DOING WHILE DOING WHAT WE MUST

What most men never come to realize, or are never told, or forget, is that they already possess a calling and purpose. One that surpasses the specific industry they're in or job they have. It's given to them by God, their creator. It is tied to who they are as men and not the particular thing they do. There are priorities that God has called them to, responsibilities that are inherent in their persons, passions imbedded in their masculinity, and commitments intrinsic to their roles as men. There's no need to search for these. They're built-in. These are larger than specific careers. Awareness of these greater realities gives the day-to-day its more sustainable meaning.

Point is, we forget what we're *actually* doing while doing what we *have* to. What is work anyway? It's not who I am. I may be a salesman, doctor, or teacher, but that is just a means to an end. It's what I do. Who I am is a husband and dad saved by grace. One simply provides the opportunity to do the other. When we confuse the means and the end we inevitably fall off one of these two edges—a want of meaning or a misplaced identity. If my greater desire is to be successful rather than faithful, I'm in trouble. It's the greater reality that keeps the other in proper perspective. As a man, you have to be gripped by the greater to survive the latter. You must keep the means and end separate.

I absolutely love being a dad. Maybe it's my particular context that makes me so intense about it. Maybe it's not abnormal to think this way. Maybe it's the way it should be. Maybe it's the way all real dads feel. Regardless, I love it. In no way am I a perfect dad. I'm still learning and adjusting. It's challenging. After all, I have a teenage daughter—the equivalent of solving a Rubik's Cube in pitch-black darkness during a typhoon. Seriously, I don't get it. But even this I love. The responsibility of being a guiding force in my kids' lives overwhelms me.

Every day I live I'm thinking of them. Praying for them. I know them and fear for them. It's a dark world out there. More than once, like many other dads, I have been found on my knees next to their beds weeping for their souls and praying for their futures.

Men are created to be on their knees beside the lives of their wife and kids. It's part of God's design. Other creatures (wives and children) are designed to depend upon this trait in us. It's imbedded in our makeup, part of the structure of the relationship between husband and wife and an important part of how we bring glory to God as men. It's not simply finances and material resources we provide. What we supply is much greater than these things. We offer hope, trust, love, stability, guidance, service, and all those intangibles that come with our roles as fathers and husbands. And these are the realities that give our lives more meaning than careers ever could.

I Think They Got It

The other night my sons attended a professional hockey game. It was a guys' night out sponsored by their school. The headmaster, several of the male teachers, and other dads escorted a group of elementary-aged boys to the game. Such madness. God bless them for doing it. After they returned home my youngest son was visibly disturbed. I could see it. He had met a new friend. At some point during the game my son's new friend disclosed his family situation. It was not good. His father was gone. He did not have one. As my son put it, "His dad did not want him and left. He is now remarried and has three other children. He never sees him."

My son, who is eight, could not make this make sense. With a very innocent level of clarity he understood the injustice. It was deeply distressing to him. "How could a dad do that?" Unfortunately, there's not an easy answer. Unfortunately, it's far too common a scenario.

In that moment I think my sons, both of them, at least for that moment, got it—how blessed they are to have a dad. (Not perfect, but present. Not perfect, but engaged.) Their reaction to this young man was similar to my mom's reaction to her own lonely little boy so many years ago. It's a hard reality to deal with.

The response in my son was love and warmth toward his own dad. He clung to me. Later he asked if he could sleep in his big brother's room in the lower bunk. It was as if he prized more highly and was drawn into more closely the bond of family and brotherhood. (It could also be that he used the situation to manipulate his dad. But that is beside the point.) He asked if we could pray for this young man. So there we were; dad, mom, brother and son, on our knees praying for the unique presence of a heavenly Father in this kid's life. We gave thanks for our own family and closed. I did my usual round of hugs and kisses and then walked out with tears in my eyes. *That* is what I live for as a dad. It's who I am. I get to be there for these boys. No one has to pity them, or cry over them as statistics.

If you took me back in time thirty minutes from that moment on my knees with my family and told me what was about to occur—how God would bless me with some of the most sincere love a man could ever experience, how I would have a chance to leave an indelible mark on my son's tender heart—if you took me back and offered me ten million dollars to miss it, I would turn you down every time. Because there are things more valuable than money and careers. Truly priceless. There are a thousand little priceless moments all around us. You only have to pay attention. You only have to love the looking. Your ability to be there in those moments has nothing to do with your career, or lack thereof. Your kids never see that stuff anyway. You're just their dad.

CLASS OFFERED AT BOYCE COLLEGE, LOUISVILLE, KY; PROFESSOR JOE POWELL

SPRING 2011, BOYCE COLLEGE

Look not mournfully into the past, it comes not back again.
Wisely improve the present, it is thine.
Go forth to meet the shadowy future without fear and with a manly heart.
{ HENRY WADSWORTH LONGFELLOW }

Hard work spotlights the character of people. Some turn up their sleeves,
some turn up their noses and some don't turn up at all.
{ SAM EWING }

I. COURSE DESCRIPTION

To identify, groom, and develop 12 solid young men at Boyce College. It has been rightly said that higher education grooms the mind, but neglects the body. It could be added that the social construct of men is designed to be developed outside of the classroom accomplishing difficult tasks amidst hard work. Many times this takes the form of sports. However, Boyce College needs to equip men in their masculinity who will in turn lead other men and develop a culture of expressed masculinity. This is an essential component of theological education and equipping for ministry.

Many Boyce College students will leave the institution uniquely equipped to debate theology, argue philosophy, and parse Greek verbs. However, the student's ability to impact culture can sometimes be undermined by a lack of knowledge about more masculine areas of interest. In their churches and workplaces they will gain credibility, broaden their impact, and increase their leadership profile if they properly learn several basic masculine skills. Many young men currently leave Boyce College ill-equipped to operate in the culture of their parishioners. As Winston Churchill rightly said, "No technical knowledge can outweigh knowledge of the humanities."

II. OFFICIAL OBJECTIVES

Develop courage, satisfaction, and proliferation in the lives of a few select men at Boyce College.

III. LEARNING OBJECTIVES

1. How to forge knives
2. How to shoot and clean guns
3. How to build fires (without a lighter)
4. How to camp...without tents
5. Go to a butcher shop and see:
   a. What cuts of meat come from where?
   b. What are better things about different cuts of meat?
   c. How to pick out a steak
   d. How to butcher beef
6. Trip to ranch
7. How to drive tractors
   a. How to use the bucket
   b. How to drive a bulldozer/bobcat
8. How to back up a trailer
9. How to use a chainsaw
10. How to split wood
11. How to shoot skeet
12. How to herd cattle
13. How to castrate a bull
14. How to string a barbed wire fence
15. How to smoke a brisket
16. How to grill
17. How to tan leather (Orrick)
18. How to build a building
    a. Pour the concrete footings/slab

    b. Frame the building

    c. Run the electricity

    d. Roof a building

19. Learn about cars

    a. How to change a flat tire

    b. How to change the oil

    c. How to put a tire on a rim

    d. How an engine works

    e. How to change brake pads

    f. What is under the hood of a car?

20. How to fly fish

21. How to shoot a bow and arrow

22. Learn all about spelunking

23. Combat first aid

24. How to rappel/climb/bouldering

25. How to scuba dive

26. How to go muddin'

27. How to whittle

28. Ride along with a police officer

29. How to navigate—with a compass

30. How to suture a wound

31. How a gun works—manufacturing

32. How to pan for gold

33. How to milk a cow

34. How to put out a fire

35. Fundamentals of hand-to-hand combat

36. Shoot all kinds of guns (shotgun, long-range rifle, carbine, pistols, automatics, etc.)

37. How to reload ammo

38. How to weld

39. How to drive a boat

40. How to drive a forklift

41. How to cook something that you kill

42. How to dress well

43. How to sharpen a knife

VI. OUTINGS

Tool overview
Car overview
Roofing overview
Roofing party
Electricity
Camping, fires, kill and eat
How to dress to kill
How to suture a wound
Guns—shooting, cleaning, etc.
Wood splitting, axes, knife sharpening
Meat—butcher shop
Grill out

18

INTEGRITY: BE THE MAN
THEY THINK YOU ARE

*The light called history is pitiless; it possesses this peculiar and divine
quality, that pure light as it is, and precisely because it is wholly
light, it often casts a shadow in places where people had hitherto
beheld rays; from the same man it constructs two different phantoms,
and the one attacks the other and executes justice on it...* [3]

{ Victor Hugo }

*To me it is a very small thing that I may be examined by you, or by any
human court; in fact, I do not even examine myself. For I am conscious
of nothing against myself, yet I am not by this acquitted; but the one
who examines me is the Lord. Therefore do not go on passing judgment
before the time, but wait until the Lord comes who will both bring
to light the things hidden in the darkness and disclose the motives of
men's hearts; and then each man's praise will come to him from God.*

{ 1 Corinthians 4:3-5 }

L osing a father to tragedy is like having a pillar in your life suddenly give way. Lifelong supports underneath your existence crack and then cave in. There is a real sense of collapse as realities fall out from under you. Grief is what happens as our heart reaches out on the way down to the hard reality of death below. He was fifty. I was twenty-six. I was in the beginning of my life. He was in the thick of his. I know it's cliché, but I really didn't know how much I loved and depended on the man until he was gone. None of us did. No one ever does. There's not a day that goes by that I do not think of him.

There were many things for which I was unprepared in those months following his death. Settling his estate was one of them. The business side of death is an uncaring visitor who shows up with his hand out at the funeral. It does not come consoling, but begging. In the middle of all your family's pain you have to find your legs and walk through countless financial decisions. Purchasing caskets. Ordering death certificates. Gathering insurance proceeds. Executing wills. Settling debts. Probate. Disbursements of properties and funds. Estate taxes. I, along with my mother and a family friend, met with bankers, financial institutions, insurance agents, and numerous other people who tried to manage the impossible gap between broken people and clients.

Courage Is a Box of Memories

As hard as all this was, no pain compared to the process of organizing my father's personal effects. Furthermore, as painful as it was for the kids, they can never really grasp the pain their mom felt. Real pain is watching my mother slowly come to the realization that shirts and shoes must be removed from closets. Real strength is her finally doing it. It's like attempting to drag a memory out of your heart. They don't go easily. They grab hold of certain objects and hang on for life. You sit reluctantly for hours staring at items that make no sense without the person who gave them meaning. Love is a woman gathering a pile of her deceased husband's dress shirts up in her arms and smelling them. Courage is boxing them up.

Inevitably, the day came when we had to close out his office. I flew to town for the occasion so as to be by my mom's side. I remember standing outside his office with her preparing to "clean it out." But do lives really fit in boxes? (I pray the totality of who I am doesn't fit in a few pathetic boxes.) That dreadful door had been closed for weeks. None of his family had stepped in that space since he'd passed. The finality involved in this task was too much to bear so we left it undone as long as we could. It was the bitter end. Few thresholds were this painful.

We stood there in the hallway outside his office looking at the plaque on the door—*Dr. Victor Yawn, MD*. I'd seen it a thousand times, but never paid that much attention to it. You pay better attention once you're on the other side of a life. We take so many small things for granted.

My entire life was in that name. By God's grace I was Dr. Victor Yawn's son. My life made no sense without it. It had been an incredible journey of grace. In sight of it my mom slid down the wall and said, "I can't go in. You have to do it." I suppose it was the weight of the moment. Some memories don't go easily and others deserve to remain undisturbed.

I stepped in and shut the door behind me. I stood face-to-face with the remainder of my dad's life. Drawers were emptied. Documents were sorted. Pictures taken down. Books removed from shelves. Cherished artifacts off his desk and credenza went into plastic containers. I had broken half of them when I was young. They were a little part of my childhood. I packed his practice up and walked it out to our Suburban box by box.

WHAT'S BEHIND A LIFE?

At the end of the day, I distinctly remember being confronted with a locked cabinet behind his desk. It struck me as odd because it was the only locked anything I had faced in dealing with the estate. In a literal sense, opening it was the very last thing I had to do in the long process of "closing up" his life.

It occurred to me at that moment that my dad's life had come down to this locked cabinet. The only thing that stood between his life and legacy was its contents. I realize such a thought is a rather dramatic oversimplification of five decades. So much more is involved in the final estimation of a man. But at the time, it was a tangible way for a son to find closure. The funeral had long been over, but this moment was the real memorial. I had a pile of little brass keys collected from the drawers in his desk. I tried ten before I came to the one that fit.

LIES AND FUNERALS

More lies are told at funerals than at any other occasion. They are forced out as the silent deceptions of a man's character are finally dealt with at his memorial service. People spend lifetimes covering or ignoring the truth of who they are. Friends and family, who spent their lives playing along with the deception while they were alive, stick to the beloved's script in the end.

In the moment of a funeral, the description bears almost no similarity to the actual people memorialized. Mourners flip the funeral program over to make sure they're in the right service. If we were half the people in life others will say we were at our funerals we might have lives that don't require such edits. It's a bizarre type of courtesy paid to the bereaved. But it's a disservice to reality. We should speak up sooner.

At that moment, when people stand over us and say nice things, the truth about who we were is already out there. They can lay a spray of kind words over reality, but it can't cover the truth about who we were.

I've preached countless funeral services throughout my ministry. The delicate balance of truthfulness and honor is a sobering responsibility. With the broken hearts of widows and children sitting a few feet from you, you weigh your words carefully. Families hand you the narrative of their loved one's life in facts, anecdotes, time lines, pictures, and memories. Your challenge is to assemble decades of a life in a few final sentences. They hand you the blank space of the final chapter of a person's life and ask you to wrap it up. But by that time the end has already been written. They were the person they were no matter what you say.

There's nothing so powerful as a life that speaks for itself. A life that is its own benediction. A life that is a translation of integrity. More than once I've thanked the deceased publicly for not forcing me to make things up at the end of their lives. You can't rewrite the endings anyway. You might ignore them out of civility, but you can't fix them. The more consistent the life, the easier the funeral is to preach. The best funeral preaches itself.

We carry the final chapter of our lives around with us every day we live. It's our next decision. We're the mosaic of every decision we've ever made. When we die we push print. *You* wrote your life's story moment by moment. Not preachers and loved ones. It's not the honorable mentions of accomplishments, or financial worth, or possessions. People will accomplish greater things than you. If you were fortunate to have any, people who "loved" you will fight over the money you leave behind. Your possessions will fit into boxes of all shapes and sizes. The real conclusion is about integrity. What kind of man you were. The last thing written about your life will be the correspondence between who people thought you were and who you actually were. What your family actually inherits is the truth.

Not long ago I preached a funeral of a patriarch in our church. He and his wife had been married for more than sixty-five years. He was a faithful man. His life preached his own funeral. I had been with him throughout his downturn as he was in and out of hospitals. There were things I wanted to say to him—words of thanks—but he was not conscious at the end. So I wrote him a letter and read it at his funeral. Here's what I wrote.

Dear Mark,

Thank you for the last ten years. But more importantly, thank you for the seventy-eight which preceded them. I realize a man is not known for individual events as much as he is for the accumulation of life. Thank you for the good ending to your narrative. And thank you for the forty years of faithfulness at Community Bible Church. Thank you for a pair of shoulders many men like myself stand on—a foundation to build on and a legacy for which to aim.

Very soon (by now no doubt) you will hear "Well done, thou good and faithful servant." But I wanted you to know the wake of good things left in your life's path. I wanted to say that you ran well and finished even better. I know that in these last days it seemed your usefulness was gone. I assure you it was not. It had only changed shapes. For you did what you could with what you had while you could. Trust me, your life will be felt many years from now.

There are souls being won to Christ today in a church whose foundation you helped lay. CBC has yet to leave its first love because you never lost yours. Many countless people have enjoyed the sweet balance of grace and truth which was a hallmark of your life. Whenever I sense it and hear the sweet fellowship of the body of Christ I hear your voice.

There are many things you have taught me. Too many to name. But I asked you once what you would do different if you had it all to do over again. Expecting something about discipline and determination, I was surprised to hear weakness, trembling, and fear. You confessed you would have prayed more often than you did. That too much was done in your own strength. Those words have rung in my ears. Ironically, if I hope to match your accomplishments I will have to turn away from my own.

Mark, I'm grateful to God that you were faithful. That you did not walk away or disgrace Christ's name. That you finished well. I know that you would object to all these things being said about you at your funeral. That is what I loved most about you—humility. You denied every good thing we mention about you here and fled to Christ while you lived. You climbed up a cross of grace and taught others how to do the same over eighty-eight years.

I wanted you to know that you had not run in vain. That if you were concerned about how you would be remembered or whether your life made a difference for the gospel, that it has, and will for many years to come. You have set the bar high and stretched the pace way out. Most of us here have wasted enough time in our lives thus far and you not a single breath.

I thank God that I did not have to make anything up about your life or explain anything of it away.

Your friend,
Byron

P.S. Dear Mark, you were gone before I could read this to you, so please ignore it and enjoy your reward.

P.P.S. I'm wearing a tie in your honor.

I pray someone can read a letter like this over my life. I pray my sons won't find a key that opens a space that sheds light on a different man from the one I professed to be.

THE JOY OF FINDING NOTHING

There was nothing in that locked cabinet in my dad's office. (By nothing, I mean medical journals.) I've never been so relieved to find nothing. Nothing is powerful at the end. He was the man I thought he was. Simple. Unassuming. Transparent. Not perfect, but consistent. I don't remember everything I said at his funeral months before this moment. What I said doesn't matter. What does matter were the contents of a cabinet. A life laid bare did not require me to amend what I said in any way.

You're going to die. Maybe tomorrow. Maybe tragically. Maybe forty years from now. Your family, in one way or another, will be faced with the task of digging around in the remains of who you were. As you are dead, there will be nothing you can do to stop them. Those defenses that kept back the truth about you while you were alive will be powerless in death. Your children will face the truth about you. They may come to discover things they never knew about you. They will face a locked cabinet of one sort or another. What will they find there?

Dear Dad, thank you for ending well.

BATMAN AND SPIDERMAN

19

AFTERWORD

Dad, were you excited when you found out you were having a boy?
{ VICTOR WADE YAWN III }

Yes, son. You have no idea how excited.
{ BYRON FORREST YAWN }

I 've never struggled with not having a connection with my biological father. When people hear of him they often ask, "Do you have a relationship with him?" Inevitably, when I answer in the negative, they assume there's some level of bitterness and regret. I realize their concern comes from a good place. But it's hard to convince them otherwise. There has to be a daddy wound in there somewhere. It's assumed that such circumstances leave irreparable damage to a person. They don't have to.

In my own case it's had a very positive effect. For one, I carry around with me this concrete sense of providence. I can't believe where I am, whom I'm married to, my three children, and what I get to do. The odds were stacked against me. But grace beats unbeatable odds every time. God has blessed me. I'm acutely aware of this every day I live.

It's also made me a more industrious father. In no way am I perfect. My kids bear the proof. Maybe having seen firsthand the importance of a father figure from both angles I view it as my primary role outside of marriage. My identity is not a pastor. My identity is Christ. And then a husband. And then a father. And then a church member. And then a pastor. I'd rather be a good husband and father than a pastor any day of the week. In fact, this prioritization is required by God. If I fail as a father and husband I have no ministry anyway. I'm far more concerned with the opinions of my wife and children toward me than I am church people. My wife and kids know far better whether I have integrity. I can mail it in on most any other level. Not with them.

Point is, despite the early going, things have fallen in good places for me. Honestly, there is no pain involved in reflecting upon my progenitor. I've had no reason to be bitter. I've never been that guy who lingered on misfortunes. When I was a kid I was happy being alive and well on the planet. I'm still somewhat that way, by God's grace alone. Life and ministry haven't completely jaded me. I'm grateful for my life.

Yet there have been times when I've wondered where things in me come from. Certain tendencies and habits had to have come from somewhere. I've got my own share of quirks that didn't come from my mom's side. These have been a curiosity from time to time. But other than the occasional fleeting thought, it's not been a big part of my existence.

Therefore, I never considered connecting with my biological father as a significant option. It's been over thirty years since I've seen him and twenty-five years since I heard his voice via a phone call. He placed it to me on my birthday. He's had his own life to live over these years. I've had my own. Thirty years is a long time.

Fifteen years after my father died in the wreck, I found myself in my biological father's hometown on a trip. Out of curiosity I contacted him and asked if he'd be interested in a cup of coffee. I was in the middle of completing this book at the time. I was in the state of mind that I could assess it all rightly. Of course, he agreed. I told my wife and kids about the meeting before I left. They were mildly curious.

We met at my hotel. Believe it or not, it wasn't awkward for me. I wasn't nervous. Thirty years is a long time. I was a man in my own right. He in his. From the start it was apparent this was not going to be a nostalgic father-son reunion, but a unique moment to fill in some gaps. When he arrived it was apparent he was nervous. I get that. Thirty years is a long time. I'm sure he expected me to go inner child on him. I guess my inner child is on Ritalin. I had none of that stuff for him.

First thing he said to me was "You look like your mother." Funny.

My mother once told me I looked just like him. We settled right in and started exchanging factoids about our respective lives. I have three half-brothers. He has three grandchildren. Those kinds of things. It was pleasant and amicable. He was extremely grateful I had looked him up. I told him it was no problem at all. I got a real sense that the entire event was a moment of long-awaited closure for him.

As I sat with him, the mystery behind many of my idiosyncrasies was solved. It was like looking into a mirror as he did certain things. The way he carried himself. The way he ate his sandwich. It was enlightening. Some closure for me as well, I suppose. We spent the better part of the morning talking.

When he dropped me back off at the hotel he said simply, "Thank you for calling me. Thank you for being the man you are." He wasn't taking credit for it. I think he was breathing a sigh of relief. He too saw the unmistakable marks of God's providence on me. God landed me on my feet.

When I arrived back home I sat down with my family at dinner and shared the details of my meeting with them. I filled my space—the space where a dad should be. As I sat there taking them in, I was looking for something specific. Having just a few hours before sat across from the man who had given me life, my mind was spinning. *I'm so glad I haven't missed this,* I thought to myself. There was something I needed to see. Something that comes with time and grace. And there it sat in four precious souls—the respect of my family. There is nothing more precious.

At the end of the day I think I'm engaged. I think I'm slightly more than "good, but not much" as a father. It is by God's grace I sit at this table at all. There are these rare moments in life when we think with absolute clarity. When we get it. When we see what's important. I saw it. I saw myself in my sons. I liked what I saw so far. Chapter closed.

I immediately got back to the business I love more than any other—being a husband and father.

Post Tenebrus Lux

Notes

1. As cited in *Christianity Today* article "Living by Vows," at www.christianitytoday.com/ct2004/februaryweb-only/2-9-11.html.

2. Tim Russert, *Wisdom of Our Fathers: Lessons and Letters from Daughters and Sons* (New York: Random House, 2006), p. xiv.

3. Victor Hugo, *Les Miserables* (New York: Thomas Y. Crowell & Co., 1887), p. 1010.

For more information about Byron's ministry go to

{ WWW.CBCNASHVILLE.ORG }

or follow him on Twitter

{ @BYRONYAWN }

*For information about how to form a
multigenerational men's ministry in your area or church, go to*

{ WWW.THETRAJECTORY.COM }

OTHER GOOD
HARVEST HOUSE READING

At the Throne of Grace
John MacArthur

As an essential part of worship for more than four decades, John MacArthur has led the congregation of Grace Community Church in prayer. For many, this has been a highlight of their Sunday worship. This book includes 54 prayers given over the course of John MacArthur's ministry and is brimming with rich inspiration for your own prayer life.

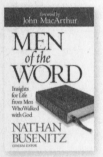

Men of the Word
Nathan Busenitz, General Editor

What is God's calling for men? What is biblical manhood, and how is it cultivated? You'll find the answers to these all-important questions in the lives of the men of the Bible—men who struggled with the same issues you face today. From them you'll learn that real men live by faith, treasure God's Word, flee temptation, refuse to compromise, lead with courage, and find satisfaction in God.

A Man After God's Own Heart
Jim George

Look at God's design for how you can become a man who has a real impact in all the key areas of your life—your marriage relationship, the parenting of your children, your work ethic and the example you set, your service at church, and your interactions with the people around you. Learn how to develop the wisdom and strength that will ensure you are a man who makes a *lasting* difference.